THE
INVISIBLE
WAR

VOLUME TWO

• • • ◆ • • •

DR. UWAKWE C. CHUKWU

DR. UWAKWE CHRISTIAN CHUKWU
Hearts of Jesus and Mary Ministries
website: www.hjamm.org
Email: ucchukwu@hjamm.org
Email: ucchukwu42@students.tntech.edu

Ordering Information
Quantity sales. Special discounts are available on quantity purchases by corporations, associations, and others. For details, contact the "Special Sales Department" at the information above.

The Invisible War (Volume 2)
Dr. Uwakwe Christian Chukwu—1st edition
ISBN: 978-1-64606-334-5

Published in the United States of America by CreateSpace

THE
INVISIBLE
WAR

VOLUME TWO

DEDICATION

·· ◆ ◆ ◆ ◆ ◆ ··

To My Wife:
Mrs Chinyere Gloria Uwakwe
She is my friend and companion in this journey of faith!

TABLE OF CONTENTS

ACKNOWLEDGMENT

· ◆ ◆ ◆ ◆ ◆ ◆ · ·

My foremost gratitude goes to the Holy Spirit who provided the inspiration, guidance, and grace to write this book. I would like to take this opportunity to thank in a very special way Miss Marie Bernadette Abe Ewongkem and one other sister (who preferred anonymity) for their wonderful editorial expertise in taking the manuscript of this book and painstakingly moderating it. I am very thankful to you all!

I am utterly grateful to my Spiritual Director and mentor, Rev. Fr. Cletus Imo. He is both my father and my model. His life inspires me much. It is largely his mentoring, combined with the support I receive from others like him that keep me aflame in the faith. A million thanks cannot suffice to express my gratitude to Rev. Fr. Anthony Madu for the sacrifices he makes in sharing the Word of God weekly in our Ministry.

Many words may be said, but none is enough to appreciate the support received from my parents, Mr. Nweke-Onovo Chukwu and Mrs. Roseline Chukwu, most especially for showing me the way to God. You have no idea of the gravity of my deeply-felt gratitude for your sacrifices that brought me thus far. Mum, you are the first prayer warrior I ever knew. You are the one who laid the foundation for my prayer life. You prayed the fire of God into my life!

I have no luxury of space to thank all the passionate and caring members of my ministry—*Hearts of Jesus and Mary Ministries* (HJM)—for their unrelenting prayers for my family and ministry. HJM family is a legion in my life, and I am filled with gratitude for their willingness in showering me with the greatest gift—prayers. I reserve a sincere gratitude to all the Board of Directors, Ministry Leaders, and Workers in the HJM Ministry, whose efforts in the ministry stir deep gratitude from my heart.

My gratitude goes to Mr. Emmanuel Aryee for taking his time to typeset this book and for designing the cover. I also appreciate the suggestions of Dr. Uzo Geoff in the back cover design.

I am overwhelmingly grateful to my beautiful wife, Chinyere, and our wonderful kids—Chiemelie, Onyinyechi, Mmesomachukwu, and Ebubechukwu—for making our family a happy home for all of us. I appreciate your prayerful supports. Many kisses from Angel-Dad! God bless you all.

I dedicate this book to you, my wife, Chinyere. You are a great friend!

FOREWORD

$\cdots \diamond \blacklozenge \diamond \cdots$

The problem of evil has been an age long one. It is as if there is something in the air about it presently. The news media has a series of witnesses of horrible violence that pervades our streets, towns, and cities. It is on the screen, in the music, in our schools, in our homes, online media and personal experiences. While sufferings can be caused by natural disasters or human errors, there is another caused by invisible forces that is sparsely spoken about by people.

Though some people in their ignorance deny the existence of invisible forces and their oppressive activities, Paul does not mince words in his teaching about the existence of satanic influences when he says: *"Put on the whole armor of God, that you may be able to stand against the wiles of the devil. For we are not contending against flesh and blood, but against the principalities, powers, the world rulers of this present darkness, and the spiritual hosts of wickedness in the heavenly places"* (Ephesians 6:11-12). Further Peter succinctly admonished believers: *"Be sober-minded and alert. Your adversary, the devil prowls around like a roaring lion, seeking someone to devour. Resist him, standing firm in your faith and in the knowledge that your brothers throughout the world are undergoing the same kinds of suffering...."* (1 Peter 5:8-9).

In this book, Bro. Uwakwe Christian Chukwu tells the reader how the invisible forces operate and how to resist and counter their attacks. One problem with our times is that a lot of people who are undergoing some difficulties attribute them to the devil when in reality it is not. Others whose misfortunes are truly caused by the devil, just because they are conscious of some direct attacks, may not know what to do about it or may be led to the wrong places where they are being taken advantage of by fake pastors or the so-called men and women of God, who use such opportunities to make money or immorally abuse their victims. In this regard, The Invisible War is a great book with moving personal testimonies of the author and those he has delivered from the power of the enemy, the devil, to possess.

In *The Invisible War*, Bro. Uwakwe sets out to explore the different sheds of satanic oppression, exposing their tricks and inner energy. He draws the attention of the reader to some experiential instances of people whose lives the devil has menaced, and/or stolen their destinies, then subject them to a prolonged hardship and torture. He also taught the reader how to engage in a spiritual battle against the wiles of the enemy of progress, the devil, through prayer and the witness of a good Christian life. He made available in this piece of information some invaluable spiritual resources for people who are personally fighting real spiritual battles in their lives, families, job places or in their relationships as well as for those who are living in bondage of sins that are difficult to break or those who through fear of death are subjected to lifelong slavery.

It is important to state here that some people need Church approved exorcists to deal with their spiritual phenomena, as these manifestations are called, but most people do not need to face exorcists, they need to face themselves and their fears. This book presents Jesus Christ, as the way out of these manifestations when they are real. It is filled with numerous stories illustrating how one can be set free by personally engaging in a twenty-one-day prayer while exercising faith in the power of the accomplished work of Jesus on the Cross. It invites the reader to discover or rediscover what the Scriptures have taught about God's love, compassion and mercy for the afflicted and His eternal promises to set them free when called upon in prayer. Bro. Uwakwe's insight and passion to help those who are undergoing spiritual attacks is revealed in this practical remedy to avert what is truly ailing humanity in real ways.

Fr. Cletus Imo, PhD

INTRODUCTION

···♦ ♦ ◆ ♦ ♦···

"A roaring lion and a charging bear that's what a wicked tyrant is over poor people."

(Proverbs 28:15, ISV)

"For [the] tyrant shall be no more, and [the] scoffer shall come to an end. And all those lying in wait for evil shall be cut off."

(Isa 29:20, LEB)

"And I will deliver you from the hand of the wicked, and I will redeem you from [the] hand of [the] tyrant."

(Jeremiah 15:21)

Every age in history have had its tyrants. They used their military and economic power to create territorial domination in order to achieve what seemed like an eternity of brutality on the people. People live in bondage when a tyrant is in charge of how their lives go. Likewise, spiritual tyrants keep people in spiritual bondage. They are the spiritual dictators, slave drivers, and wicked master bullies. They torment, and by doing so they derive pleasure to see suffering spelled in the faces of people. They want you in spiritual confinement forever. Do you wonder why all hell breaks loose when you realize the truth and want your freedom? They come to fight with great fury when their captives are receiving the light of freedom. They don't want you free!

Stories of men and women performing deeds of valor on the spiritual battlefield didn't end in the Bible times or with the lives of saints from centuries past. Jesus Christ needs people who are willing to put on the full armor of God, push back lines defined by the kingdom of darkness, and advance the kingdom of God here on earth.

Jesus' story of the thief in the night brings home the character of the spiritual tyrant that comes uninvited, especially under the cover of darkness and secrecy! Lurking in the haze of darkness, they seek to master every heart and soul on the face of the earth. In the volume 1 of this book, we saw that these spirits can be very brutal. However, because they are invisible, most people downplay or even ignore their existence.

My dear friend, there is a fierce spiritual battle or an invisible war over your destiny! According to **Ephesians 6:12** *"Our struggle is not against enemies of blood and flesh, but against the rulers, against the authorities, against the cosmic powers of this present darkness, against the spiritual forces of evil in the heavenly places."* Considering the fact that the outcome of this invisible war will determine our destiny, it is essential that we identify the devil's deadly devices and proactively confront him and his kingdom with our prayers. You must fight the enemy, else you can't fulfill your destiny! The battle is serious enough to cause God to send His only Son, Jesus Christ, to die the most painful death ever—just to deliver your destiny from the captivity of the spiritual tyrants! The Lord God promises: *"And I will deliver you from the hand of the wicked, and I will redeem you from [the] hand of [the] tyrant."* (Jeremiah 15:21)

The spiritual tyrants are responsible for every demonic oppression (like the woman crippled for eighteen years in **Luke 13:11–13**), every demonic possession (like the demoniac man described in **Mark 5:2–8** as living in the tombs with unclean spirits in him), and most cases of obsession (frightening dreams, uncontrollable evil thoughts, spirits that cling to emotional wounds or unhealthy relationships, and hallucinations). Although the Bible contains many works or activities of the tyrants, we shall pay close attention to the *"enormous red dragon"* described in **Revelation 12:3.**

The Bible vividly presents the spiritual tyrant to us in **Revelation 12:3-4** as *"an enormous red dragon with seven heads and ten horns and seven crowns on its heads. Its tail swept a third of the stars out of the sky and flung them to the earth."* Its saliva is like a river capable of sweeping an adult away—*"Then from his mouth, the serpent poured water like a river after the woman, to sweep her away with the flood"* (**Revelation 12:15**).

What a figure of the spiritual tyrant defined! We get an idea of the momentous wickedness of this invisible force as he stood like a warrior before a pregnant woman who *"was crying out in birth pangs, in the agony of giving birth"* (**Revelation 12:2**). Do you think he was there as a midwife to assist her in childbirth? No! He was there to kill! **Revelation 12:4** says he *"stood before the woman who was about to bear a child so that he might devour her child as soon as it was born."* In **Revelation 12:5,** God intervened and saved the woman and her male child that she gave birth to. *"Then the dragon was angry with the woman,"* and goes after her and the true Church—*"those who keep the commandments of God and hold the testimony of Jesus"* (**Revelation 12:17**). There is, for sure, a defined spiritual war against the Body of Christ, the true Church.

The "red dragon" is in a determined mission to *"lead the whole world astray"* (**Revelation 12:9, NIV**). The devil knows that the Church is our place of refuge, so he goes to attack the Church and *"blinding the minds of men from the Gospel of Jesus"* (**2 Corinthians 4:4**). As the Scripture tells us, the devil prowls around like a roaring lion looking for someone to devour (**1 Peter 5:8**). He came after the woman and the destiny of her seed. He also comes after God's people and all that they stand for in order to destroy their God-assigned mission on earth. Think of Job: he came after him and everyone in his household, resulting in the loss of all Job's children and his possessions. The suddenness of the enemy's attack on Job's family highlights the swiftness and the affinity of the spiritual tyrants to strike people uninvitedly.

Lack of vigilance in prayer is definitely an invitation for defeat when the tyrant comes! This is why Jesus Christ tells us in **Luke 21:36** to *"Be alert at all times."* Therefore, the necessity of a careful watchfulness cannot be overemphasized. We are supposed to stay spiritually alert to avert the danger of the tyrant's plunder. We cannot afford to leave the doors of our homes open for the spiritual tyrants to walk in freely to take over and take away our children, our marriage and our treasures from the family. We have to prayerfully keep our inheritance secure at all times! It is our responsibility to use the weapon of prayer to protect our families, relationships, talents, resources, and treasures lest the enemy hijacks our blessings.

James 4:7 says, *"Resist the devil, and he will flee from you."* In other words, persistence in prayer breaks the enemy's resistance! The reason why the devil gets through with his evil plans against the Church is because we are not causing him enough trouble or resistance with our prayers. Spiritual war rages on, and as soldiers of Christ, a retreat is not an option. We have to fight with prayer! Remember, if there are people to pray, there is a God to answer!

Therefore, this book offers to lead you into a spiritual warfare that causes the enemy to flee from you. It is full of prayers and information that will help you meaningfully engage the enemy in a spiritual battle that comes your way. You can use it to fight the spiritual tyrants in your family or in your Parish, workplace, school, neighborhood, city, society, or country. I encourage you to add this book to your personal library as an available resource to prepare and equip you in spiritual warfare. Our children need to read this book. Table 1 shows the recommended prayer program to fight every spiritual tyrants that are fighting against you.

Table 1

A 21 – DAY PRAYER PROGRAM USING THIS BOOK

DAY	CHAPTER TO STUDY AND PRAY WITH	FASTING PERIOD
Day 1	Introduction	
Day 2	Chapter 1: Let God Fight the Tyrant (Part 1)	
Day 3	Chapter 1: Let God Fight the Tyrant (Part 2)	
Day 4	Chapter 2: Weapons Against the Spiritual Tyrants (Part 1)	12:00am to 1:00pm
Day 5	Chapter 2: Weapons Against the Spiritual Tyrants (Part 2)	
Day 6	Chapter 3: Brace up Against the Tyrants (Part 1)	
Day 7	Chapter 3: Brace up Against the Tyrants (Part 2)	
Day 8	Chapter 4: Never Surrender! (Part 1)	
Day 9	Chapter 4: Never Surrender! (Part 2)	
Day 10	Chapter 5: Take Authority and Crush them (Part 1)	
Day 11	Chapter 5: Take Authority and Crush them (Part 2)	
Day 12	Chapter 6: Summon that Tyrant! (Part 1)	
Day 13	Chapter 6: Summon that Tyrant! (Part 2)	12:00am to 3:00pm
Day 14	Chapter 7: Return Fire for Fire (Part 1)	
Day 15	Chapter 7: Return Fire for Fire (Part 2)	
Day 16	Chapter 8: Operation Overtake the Tyrants (Part 1)	
Day 17	Chapter 8: Operation Overtake the Tyrants (Part 2)	
Day 18	Chapter 9: Divine Deliverance (Part 1)	
Day 19	Chapter 9: Divine Deliverance (Part 2)	
Day 20	Chapter 10: Overthrow the Tyrants (Part 1)	12:00am to 6:00pm
Day 21	Chapter 10: Overthrow the Tyrants (Part 2)	

Someone is in need of being rescued from the death grip of the spiritual tyrants—and Jesus is on a rescue mission to meet His child in captivity. Are you the one? I mean, are you the one that He has in mind for bringing this book into mankind? I am glad that you have this book in your hands! This book brings out a sound proof of the real existence of invisible demonic forces supported by Scriptural references. It equally elaborates in great detail the way these demonic forces afflict human life. I pray that you find this book uplifting!

This present volume (Volume 2) of *"The Invisible War"* deals with confronting the spiritual tyrants. The spiritual exercises and deliverance prayers in this prayer manual will help you and your family members push back the enemy lines and tear down demonic strongholds. Reading my earlier book titled *"War against Python & Snake Spirits"* will give you a deeper knowledge on the operations of the spiritual tyrants that possess serpentine nature. It is a book that you need in this age to arm yourself with knowledge on how to tactically fight the kingdom of darkness. The serpentine kingdom is deep—in fact very deep with unimaginable mysteries! I mention this book here because I want you to read it.

Before you read any further, I ask the Holy Spirit, Who solely inspired the writing of this book, to use it to release upon you the victor's oil that He put on David that made him destroy Goliath forever —and by the same unction, may He make you a tyrant killer henceforth! It is my prayer that through this book, you shall testify with the Psalmist in **Psalm 18:17**— *"He delivered me from my strong enemy, and from those who hated me; for they were too mighty for me."* May the defeat of the enemies be brutal such that those tyrants shall never rise again to torment you, in the name of Jesus Christ—Amen!

As I mentioned earlier in the volume 1 of this book, the ministry of God's Archangels is very important in your accomplishing victory through the prayers presented in this book. God created His Angels to help us in our times of need. The Archangel Michael who helped Daniel to overcome the prince of Persia (a spiritual tyrant) obstructing his blessings shall also be employed in this prayer to help you defeat every spiritual tyrant working against your own breakthrough. Archangel Michael is a powerful Angel skilled in fighting spiritual tyrants. We know that he was the powerful Angel that led the army of the Holy Angels who cast Satan, the chief tyrant, out of heaven with all his rebellious angels **(Revelation 12:7)**. Being guaranteed of the procession of the Armies of God's Angels on your side is enough to strengthen your faith in God as you pray.

Therefore, we shall be using St. Michael the Archangel prayer to invite the help of Archangel Michael and his other warring Angels. We shall engage St. Michael during the warfare prayers stipulated in the prayer points of every chapter of this book.

Also, we shall daily pray the prayer of *Anima Christi* (Latin for "Soul of Christ"). This is a great prayer that can prepare our soul to articulate everything we could ever need to ask of Christ, even in times of great trial. These two prayers (St. Michael and *Anima Christi*) are presented here for a quick reference, thus:

THE SAINT MICHAEL THE ARCHANGEL PRAYER

St. Michael the Archangel,
defend us in battle.
Be our defense against the wickedness and snares of the devil.
May God rebuke him, we humbly pray,
and do thou,
O Prince of the heavenly hosts,
by the power of God,
thrust into hell Satan,
and all the evil spirits,
who prowl about the world
seeking the ruin of souls. Amen.

— **Pope Leo XIII**

THE ANIMA CHRISTI PRAYER
(SOUL OF CHRIST)

Soul of Christ, sanctify me;
Body of Christ, save me;
Blood of Christ, inebriate me;
Water from the side of Christ, wash me;
Passion of Christ, strengthen me;
O good Jesus, hear me;
Within Your wounds, hide me;
Let me never be separated from You;
From the evil one, protect me;
At the hour of my death, call me;
And bid me to come close to You;
That with Your saints, I may praise You
Forever and Ever. Amen."

— Unknown

NOTE: If you are a Catholic, you are encouraged to consider receiving the Sacraments of reconciliation (confession) and Holy Communion either during or before you begin praying using this book.

DAY 1

Warfare Prayers

1. Praise and worship God as the Holy Spirit leads you.

2. Ask God for the forgiveness of your sins. Make a brief self-examination, asking the Holy Spirit to reveal every unconfessed sin. Then make the following prayers, in the name of Jesus Christ:
   a. I open all the secret places of my heart to You, O Lord Jesus. Holy Spirit, bring me to the place of deeper conversion to the Person of Jesus Christ;
   b. "Loving Father, I am sorry for all the ways I have offended You, knowingly or unknowingly. I have sinned in thoughts, words, and deeds. I have sinned in what I have done, and in what I have failed to do. I come before You and ask for the grace of a deeply repentant heart. You know my innermost secrets. I open my heart to You today and ask You to show me the ways I have blocked the flow of Your love. Forgive me, Father, for all my sins, faults and failings. For all the times I have gone astray and not chosen life, I am deeply sorry. I repent of lack of faith, acting in fear instead of faith, unbelief in Your goodness, or lack of truly believing in Your love for me." (Linda Schubert);
   c. Dear Lord Jesus Christ, please forgive me for all the times I have not submitted to Your Most Holy will in my life;
   d. Pray **Psalm 51** for the forgiveness of your sins.

3. Lord Jesus, as I go through this 21 days prayer program (pray in the name of Jesus Christ):
   a. Please draw me into a closer intimacy with You;
   b. Please send Your Angels to deal decisively with all demonic spirits (and their devices) that had access to me;
   c. Please, establish a hedge of protection around me, over

me, and under me;

    d. Please, seal me and my family with Your Most Precious Blood.

4. I now choose to put on the full armor of God, in the name of Jesus Christ.

5. I now break all agreements with the devil in the name of Jesus Christ.

6. In the name of the Lord Jesus Christ, I rebuke Satan and bind all his evil spirits along with all the princes of terrors in the air, water, fire, ground, netherworld, underground, and all other evil forces in high places.

7. Begin to decree the following in the name of Jesus Christ:
    a. Nothing shall stop my testimonies through this prayer;
    b. I take authority over all demonic engagements through this prayer.

8. Pray **Psalm 54** (make the prayers personal).

9. Pray the Saint Michael the Archangel prayer *(see above for the prayer)*.

10. Pray the Anima Christi prayer *(see above for the prayer)*.

11. I cover this prayer with the Most Precious Blood of Jesus Christ (7 times).

Chapter 1

LET GOD FIGHT THE TYRANTS

"For the Lord has driven out before you great and strong nations; and as for you, no one has been able to withstand you to this day. One of you puts to flight a thousand, since it is the Lord your God who fights for you, as he promised you."

(Joshua 23:9-10)

"Hezekiah took the letter from the hand of the messengers and read it; then he went up to the temple of the Lord, and spreading it out before Him, he prayed in the Lord's presence."

(2 Kings 19:14)

"The Lord will fight for you, and you have only to keep still."

(Exodus 14:14)

(Other suggested Bible passages to read: Exodus 14:1-31,
2 Chronicles 20:12-17, 1 Samuel 17:1-58, Psalm 91:1-16, Amos 1:1-15,
Isaiah 42:13, Isaiah 45:2, Isaiah 52:12, Deuteronomy 9:3, Isaiah
49:25, 2 Thessalonians 1:6, Deuteronomy 33:27, Proverbs 20:22,
Genesis 12:3, Psalm 129:2, Psalm 18:47, Psalm 35:1, Psalm 9:3,
Jeremiah 1:8, Psalm 7:11, 1 Samuel 2:9, Isaiah 41:11, Isaiah 59:19,
Psalm 20:6, Psalm 138:7, Psalm 44:3, Habakkuk 3:12,
Psalm 34:17, Deuteronomy 3:21)

DAY 2
Part 1: Reflection

You can't stop the devil from attacking you, but you can stop him from winning. How? By letting God fight for you. If you are in Christ, then you are following a victorious King who overthrows the usurping tyrant of the world whose shadows linger as he seeks to enforce his defunct authority. Jesus Christ has toppled and destroyed the devil's power, rescuing us from the tyrant's iron fist, settling his legal demands over us, and halting his centuries of charges **(Colossians 2:14-15)**. So my dear, no matter the length and breadth of the battle you go through now, don't fight it with your strength; let the Lord fight the battle that belongs to Him for the battle is the Lord's **(2 Chronicles 20:15)**. Yes, the battle is His, but the victory is ours. We prove that we have given Him the battle to fight when we totally surrender our lives and the situations we are going through into His mighty hands.

We, therefore, fight from victory to victory because Christ has defeated the devil on the Cross long ago. We don't fight for victory! Jesus gave us victory before the fight. David went against Goliath, but God fought the battle. He already had victory before the battle began. Always remember that God promises us in **Isaiah 49:25-26** that He will fight for us, taking the enemy captive —thus:

> *"But thus says the LORD: 'Even the captives of the mighty shall be taken, and the prey of the tyrant be rescued; for I will contend with those who contend with you, and I will save your children. I will make your oppressors eat their own flesh and they shall be drunk with their own blood as with wine. Then all flesh shall know that I am the LORD your Savior, and your Redeemer, the Mighty One of Jacob'"*

You can't beat the above promise! God has a track record of proven victories for His people who seek His help in their situations. David knew that the same God who delivered him from the lion and the bear would not fail to deliver him from Goliath. Saul tried arming David with some armor but David remembered that he was not wearing any armor when God gave him victory over the lion and the bear. God, Himself, fights armor-free! He is *"a Man of war* (Exodus 15:3, NKJV)". In fact, He Himself is the Armor: *"His eyes were like a flame of fire, His feet were like burnished bronze, refined as in a furnace, and His voice was like the sound of many waters...from his mouth came a sharp, two-edged sword, and his face was like the sun shining with full force"* (Revelation 1:14-16). Would you wonder why John testified in **Revelation 1:17** saying, *"When I saw him, I fell at His feet as though dead"?*

David knew that God was going to do the fighting for Him and that victory would be his again. Surely, David remembered the faithfulness of God in the past and believed Him for the present situation. While it is important in the battles that we go through to learn from the victory stories of other people, it's more important to look back and see the victories that God has given to us personally.

Are you facing a kind of storm that makes you want to back down? I wish to tell you that the storm is simply a sign that, help is on the way. It was when Jesus was on His way to fight the battle of the Gerasene demoniac living in the cemetery that terrible storm arose which threatened to sink the boat carrying Jesus and His disciples (**Mark 4:35-41, 5:1-17**). The storm arises when the devil sees that help is coming your way. We are quick to see the storm, but we hardly see it as a sign that Jesus is on the way. My friend, listen: the storm is a sign that the kingdom of darkness has seen God coming to fight for you—and has sent the storm to intercept that deliverance mission. The times of the storm is the season during which you should pray the most! So what should you do when the storm comes against you? Pray! What if the storm rises higher? Then, pray more! The truth is that God uses our prayers to fight our battles.

Perchance, things may have gone horribly wrong and there are stings of abandonment all around you. Help is on the way! Or maybe you are threatened by powerful enemies and distressed by God's seeming prolonged apathy and absence. Help is on the way! Who knows whether you may have already started feeling like being forsaken by God in the time of your greatest need for Him. Even so, help is on the way! *"How long, Lord?"*— you seem to question if God would ever come to your rescue **(Psalm 13: 1–2).** My dear, help is on the way! Yet, even in the face of these trials, you should run to God for only Him can bring you out of the most tragic events you may be going through right now. **Romans 8:37** reminds us that in all these things, right in the middle of all of them—trouble, hardship, persecution, famine, nakedness, danger, and even death—we are more than conquerors through Christ. This does not mean that life would be a piece of cake or a bed of roses as we want it (there's a cross to carry too as followers of Christ). But it means that the devil is not in charge because God is fighting for us in every battle. It means that our God is working out our good and packaging victory for us in every situation.

Let me tell you something: crises always reveal our character and the level of our trust in God. Although long accustomed to the brutality of the tyrant, we should not succumb to the pressure of these invisible wicked forces. Rather, we should let God help us triumph over any obstacle that we face. By leaning on God's power every time and everywhere we go, we shall have the dumbfounding victory that awaits those who let God fight their battles. The enemy cannot take hold of you if you trust and hope in God—even if the situation lingers. God may not come early, but He won't be late. So when you are waiting for answers to your prayers, believe that your help is on the way!

"What, then, shall we say in response to these things? If God is for us, who can be against us?" **(Romans 8:31, NKJV).** Personalize it and say that with me now: *"If God is for me, who can be against me?"* (You may say it 7 times!) If you really believe this, then there's no battle for you to fight because you have given it to the Lord Himself. Now, let me ask you: Which battle are you fighting now? If really you have handed the battle to the Lord, then your response should be: *"There is no battle for me to fight for I have given it to God to fight for me..."* Good! What would you say to those mountains threatening your life? You might as well say, "There is no mountain for me to fight for I have given the mountain to God to crush into dust..." You got it! Now, if you really believe what you are saying, then join me to declare with Zerubbabel (replacing Zerubbabel with your name): *"What are you, O great mountain? Before Zerubbabel you shall become a plain"* **(Zechariah 4:7).** You might as well tell the mountain your own version of **Romans 8:31**—"If God is for me, who are you mountain to be against me!"

If you think that the battle is the roughest, then just know that the victory is nearest. If you persevere a little more, you would witness the colossal collapse of the enemy under his own weight. Trapped between the sea and Pharaoh's army, the situation of the Israelites looked very hopeless: moving forward would cause them to be drowned in the Red Sea; retreating would mean ending up in the hands of the Egyptians. It was indeed a terrible situation! Yet, God assured them in **Exodus 14:13–14:**

> *"Do not be afraid, stand firm, and see the deliverance that the Lord will accomplish for you today; for the Egyptians whom you see today, you shall never see again. The Lord will fight for you, and you have only to keep still."*

Did God deliver His promise? Yes! We know that God intervened, split the sea, and brought His people safely to the other side.

This is what He wants to do for you too, only if you would trust in Him for that! God makes a way, even where there was none! No matter how wicked the plans of the enemies are, God is always there to strengthen and help His children who call upon Him for help. In the midst of any spiritual battle you might go through, you shall rise up as a warrior if the Lord God is fighting for you. Satan and his army of darkness have power—for sure—but they do not have a chance when the Lord is on our side! Hear me again: they don't have any iota of a chance!

Indeed, the attacks on you are a sign that the devil is worried about you. God has already judged and condemned the devil. So, don't give up! Don't give up the fight because God is with you always. I know that is true because He says so and His Word is Truth— *"Don't be afraid, for I am with you"* (Isaiah 41:10). He also repeatedly says this same truth several times in the Bible— enough for every day of the year, I believe! He definitely means it and wants us to believe His promises. Therefore, believe God even when everything seems to be going wrong; believe Him even in the biggest challenge and in the most turbulent of times.

Victory takes place when God is the One fighting your battle! When God fights your battle, whatever fights you, not only fights in vain but obeys you. Pharaoh obeyed Moses. The lion obeyed Daniel. The storm obeyed Jesus. The fire obeyed Shadrach, Meshach, and Abednego. The viper's poison obeyed Apostle Paul and could not harm him **(Acts 28:3-6).** Perhaps, like Daniel or Paul, you are in a battle that seems as if you are locked up in a spiritual prison with no apparent way out. You are simply one decision away from having your victory: Take courage and hand over the matter to God in prayer. Let Him fight the matter out. You can't handle it yourself! God is still in the business of making ways of escape for His children! Peter assures us that, *"the Lord knows how to rescue the godly from trial"* **(2 Peter 2:9).** God already knows how to deliver you from that totally despairing situation.

So, which battle do you need to give to God and let him fight for you? Now, before we conclude this chapter, I am going to ask you to do a simple hands-on-project that I feel comfortable to call *"burning the mountain."* This is the project:

> *Get a piece of paper. Write down each of your biggest battles on each paper and roll it into a ball (for example, write sickness on a small paper rolled into a small ball; fear of divorce written on another paper and rolled up...then same for barrenness, miscarriage, joblessness, poverty, and so on). Bring all the balls of battles or problems together. If you have so many battles going on in your life, you must have ended up having a mountain heap of balls—or call it a mountain of troubles. Perhaps your own mountain is so huge that you wouldn't see the person in front of you! Now, like King Hezekiah in 2 Kings 19:14 who took King Sennacherib's threat letter to God in prayer, you are also going to hand the mountain over to the Lord* **"Who touches the mountains and they smoke"** **(Psalm 104:32)** *and whose Presence "turns the rock into a pool of water"* **(Psalm 114:8).**

If you have faith like King Hezekiah, then that mountain is no more yours to fight but the Lord's to battle against. While facing the mountain of problems, go through the prayer points in the prayer session of this chapter and watch the Lord deal with the mountain, saying to it:

> *"I, the Lord, am your enemy. I will take hold of you, level you to the ground, and leave you in ashes"*
> **(Jeremiah 51:25, GNT)**

Do you notice the Lord saying to the mountain: "I will...*leave you in ashes*"? That's what you need! Let the Lord Jesus turn the mountains in your life to ashes. Burn the mountain and dispose of the ashes after praying, "Jesus, I trust in You" (3 times). You must have concluded the prayer points below. In the eyes of faith, see a heap of ashes, not mountains anymore. Burnt mountains are dead problems, you know. They are dead! So with your mouth, begin to confess the opposite of what used to be the mountains in your life (remember: they are no more yours but the Lord's). May the Lord confirm your faith in Jesus Christ's most glorious name. Amen!

LET US PRAY!

1. Reflect on how this reflection on "Let God Fight the Tyrants" ministers to you.
   a. Perhaps, the situations in our life today seem too far gone for redemption. Doctors may have given up on you. Death has been declared as the verdict. Yet, even at that, God can bring a turnaround: things meant for bad in your life can change for good. The Lord says to you in **Jeremiah 32:27, "See, I am the Lord, the God of all flesh; is anything too hard for me?"** Do you believe that whatever you are passing through now is nothing before God? What is it that you have stopped praying for because you haven't seen results in so long? All it takes to arrest that stubborn situation is a touch of the Lord!
   b. Pray: Father, You are the Lord. You alone are my God! You are God over everything in my sphere and beyond! There is nothing too hard for You! No situation I go through is hard for You to deal with! Like a wax, they melt before Your Presence **(Psalm 68:2)**! So, Lord, I leave this situation for You to deal with.

2. Pray the Saint Michael the Archangel prayer (see page 17).

3. Pray the Anima Christi prayer (see page 18).

4. Pray **Psalm 17** for God's deliverance from affliction.

5. The battle is the Lord's **(2 Chronicles 20:15)**, but the victory is mine— in the name of Jesus Christ. Therefore, in the name of Jesus Christ:
   a. I fight from victory to victory because Christ has defeated the devil on the Cross long ago (Jesus gave me victory before the fight!);
   b. I share in the victory of Jesus Christ over the enemy on the Cross.

6. The Bible says in **Isaiah 49:25-26**, *"But thus says the LORD: 'Even the captives of the mighty shall be taken, and the prey of the tyrant be rescued; for I will contend with those who contend with you, and I will save your children. I will make your oppressors eat their own flesh and they shall be drunk with their own blood as with wine. Then all flesh shall know that I am the LORD your Savior, and your Redeemer, the Mighty One of Jacob.'"* Therefore, I claim every promise of God in **Isaiah 49:25-26** as I begin to pray (pray the following in the name of Jesus Christ):
   a. O Lord Jesus, fight for me and take every enemy captive;
   b. O Lord Jesus, let *"the prey of the tyrant be rescued"*;
   c. O Lord Jesus, *"contend with those who contend with"* me;
   d. O Lord Jesus, save my household from the tyrants;
   e. O Lord Jesus, let the *"oppressors eat their own flesh"*;
   f. O Lord Jesus, let the *"oppressors...be drunk with their own blood;*

7. **Exodus 14:13-14** says, *"Do not be afraid, stand firm, and see the deliverance that the Lord will accomplish for you today; for the Egyptians whom you see today, you shall never see again. The Lord will fight for you, and you have only to keep still."* Therefore, I claim every promise of God in **Exodus 14:13-14** as I decree (pray the following in the name of Jesus Christ):
   a. That I am not afraid of the devil and his armies;
   b. That today, I shall "see the deliverance that the Lord will accomplish for" me through this prayer;

    c. That I shall stand firm in this fight and will not lose my peace because the Lord shall give me victory;

    d. That the tyrants I see today I shall not see again;

    e. That I shall rise up as a warrior because the Lord God is fighting for me.

8. Thank the Lord and cover this prayer with the Most Precious Blood of Jesus Christ (7 times).

DAY 3
Part 2: Warfare Prayers

Note:

- A spiritual war is a fight without mercy! You stand no chances of winning the battle on your own. God must be the One to fight for you. However, only as you pray shall God take over the fight. God works with our prayers! John Wesley once said, "God does nothing but by prayer, and everything with it."

- Your victory over the enemy confronting you is tied to your decision to allow God to do the fight. Be encouraged that no situation is beyond repair as God Himself fights for you. Let God fight the tyrants!

1. Lord Jesus Christ, I desire to see the spiritual realm as I praise and worship You in songs. Use songs to invite God the Father, Jesus the Son and the Holy Spirit.

2. Pray **Psalm 51** for the forgiveness of your sins.

3. Pray the prayer of Saint Michael the Archangel (see page 17).

4. **Jeremiah 33:3** says *"Call to me and I will answer you and will tell you great and hidden things that you have not known."* Pray the following adding *"in the name of Jesus Christ"* after each prayer.
   a. Holy Spirit, I call on Your anointing to come on me with power, authority and dominion;
   b. Holy Spirit, I pray that You anoint me with what I need to be set free through this prayer;
   c. Lord Jesus, I am calling out to You today to show me the hidden holds the enemy has over my life and my family.

5. Lord Jesus, take my battle and give me victory (pray in the name of Jesus Christ):
   a. I take authority over every unclean spirit fighting me;
   b. I strip the enemies of their weapons of warfare;
   c. The gates of hell shall not prevail against me in this prayer;
   d. I plead the Most Holy Precious Blood of Jesus Christ over this prayer and over the atmosphere of this prayer. I key into Christ's victory over the devil on the Cross of Calvary. Upon it, I stand to declare victory over the invisible forces fighting my life.

6. I stand on God's promises in **Psalm 91:1** to decree that I abide under the shadow of the Almighty God. I command every shadow of the devil seeking to cover me to be shattered — in the name of Jesus Christ.

7. I stand on God's promises in Psalm 91:2 to decree that the Lord is my Warrior: *"He is my refuge and my fortress...in Him, I will trust."*

8. I decree that..... (*pick from the following list*) in my life be completely destroyed—in the name of Jesus Christ.

- Every satanic enforcement
- All satanic legal demands
- All centuries of satanic charges
- The tyrant's iron fist
- Every affliction
- Every devils power

9. Remember when God delivered you from the enemies in the past (ask the Holy Spirit to bring past victories to your mind)?
   a. I believe that God Who delivered me from my enemies in the past shall surely deliver me in this present situation that I am going through—in the name of Jesus Christ;
   b. I shall soon share my success story—in the name of Jesus Christ;
   c. I won't give up the fight for the Lord Jesus Christ is on my side.

10. In the face of every trial, I am more than a conqueror through Christ **(Romans 8:37)** —in the name of Jesus Christ.

11. **Zechariah 4:7** says, *"What are you, O great mountain? Before Zerubbabel you shall become a plain."* What is the *"great mountain"* before you? Declare **Zechariah 4:7** unto your life by replacing Zerubbabel with your name. Then proceed as follows (praying radically the following in the name of Jesus Christ):
    a. I command the mountains to smoke as God touches them through this prayer **(Psalm 104:32)**;
    b. I command the rocks of the mountains to turn into a pool of water according to **Psalm 114:8**;
    c. The Lord says to the mountain: *"I, the Lord, am your enemy. I will take hold of you, level you to the ground, and leave you in ashes"* **(Jeremiah 51:25, GNT)**;
    d. I declare you burnt mountains dead!

12. As Pharaoh obeyed Moses, the lion obeyed Daniel, and the storm obeyed Jesus, so shall every tyrant fighting against me obey me, in the name of Jesus Christ.

13. Today I break free from the shackles of death! Today, I walk out free from every spiritual prison, in the name of Jesus Christ.

a. God says of you: *"Your covenant with death will be annulled; your agreement with the realm of the dead will not stand"* (Isaiah 28:18, NIV)—make it your own prayer by personalizing it;

b. *"Devise your strategy, but it will be thwarted; propose your plan, but it will not stand, for God is with us"* (Isaiah 8:10, NIV)—make it your own prayer by personalizing it.

14. O Holy Spirit, grant me the grace to live my life, from today, in a way that shows that I have surrendered every battle to God. Therefore, in the name of Jesus Christ, I will daily…. (pick from the following list)

- Put my complete trust in God
- Offer God my thanksgiving
- Expect my victory
- Rejoice in the Lord
- Sing praise to God
- Pray to God
- Wait on the lord to finish His battle
- Say "Yes" to Jesus with all my heart

15. Pray that the Lord visits you with a double reward for all your troubles:

a. *"And the Lord restored the fortunes of Job when he had prayed for his friends; and the Lord gave Job twice as much as he had before"* (Job 42:10). Now pray that as God fights for you, may He give you *"twice as much as [you] had before"* (Job 42:10): Double your prayer life, double your health, double your marital joy, double your peace, double your finances, double in your business, double in your family…in the name of Jesus Christ!

b. *"Instead of your shame you shall have double honor, and instead of confusion, they shall rejoice in their portion. Therefore, in their land, they shall possess double"* (Isaiah 61:7, NKJV). Make the following prayers in the name of Jesus Christ:

i. Instead of shame, I will receive a double portion;

ii. Instead of dishonor, I will rejoice in my inheritance;

iii. I will inherit a double portion in this land!

16. Meditate on **Isaiah 43:1-4** and see how committed God is in keeping you in a state of permanent victory:
    a. Thank You Lord Jesus Christ, for my permanent victory granted through this prayer— in the name of Jesus Christ;
    b. Thank You, Lord Jesus Christ, for permanently defeating all the spiritual tyrants attacking me all these years;
    c. Lord Jesus Christ, I thank You for setting me free;
    d. Sing songs of victory with **Psalm 100** and **Psalm 138.**

17. I cover this prayer with the Most Precious Blood of Jesus Christ (7 times).

Chapter 2
WEAPONS AGAINST THE SPIRITUAL TYRANTS

· ◆ ◆ ◆ ◆ ◆ ◆ ·

"For the weapons of our warfare are not carnal, but mighty through God to the pulling down of strongholds."

(2 Corinthians 10:4).

(Other suggested Bible passages to read:
2 Corinthians 10:3-6, Ephesians 6:14-18, 2 Chronicles 20:5-30,
Mark 16:17-18, Luke 10:17-20, 2 Kings 1:9-15, Exodus 10:22-23,
Psalm 91:11-12, 2 Chronicles 32:21, 2 Kings 19:35, Psalm 144:1,
Revelation 12:11).

DAY 4
Part 1: Reflection

One of America's deadliest wars was the Vietnam War. Americans took their highly sophisticated weapons to Vietnam but suffered a mind-blowing casualty from their enemies who hid on trees and inside the water using breathing apparatuses. They were hitting the Americans from their hiding places! The Americans could not even understand the strategy of the enemies that they came to fight against. The Americans were dying in great numbers as the Vietnamese prevailed against them. You see, the Vietnamese simply out-witted the Americans although the Americans had highly sophisticated technological weapons. Eventually, the Americans abandoned the war and went home. Any enemy that you do not know quite well is stronger than you! You may have advanced weapons of warfare but one of the lessons that the American-Vietnam War teaches us is that we should properly investigate the strengths of our enemy.

In the same manner, if we Christians do not understand the kind of battle that we are in, then we would be rendered useless and defeated. Granted that God has given us the superior weapons of warfare that we need in order to win every spiritual battle confronting us daily, but we are overcome by the enemies if we are outwitted by the enemies (**2 Corinthians 2:11** says, *"And we do this so that we may not be outwitted by Satan; for we are not ignorant of his designs")*. The situation is worse if we go to war (actually we are in a constant raging spiritual war) but we don't know how to use the weapons of warfare. We are disadvantaged when we have not effectively understood nor efficiently utilized God's spiritual weapons at our disposal to successfully fight the spiritual enemy of our lives. It is clear that we are called as a Body of Christ to fight and defeat the devil and his parade of spiritual tyrants through the weapons given to us.

One other lesson that a Christian ought to learn from America-Vietnam War is that spiritual warfare requires a good offense, a good defense, and effective intelligence. Effective intelligence is necessary not only to study the enemy and his operations very well but also to make tactical and strategic attacks and defenses. Proper intelligence reduces casualties.

We see the power of a good intelligence reconnaissance when in May 2011, the US Navy SEALs carried out an operation that killed Osama bin Laden, the leader of Al-Qaeda terrorist's group.

The Central Intelligence Agency (CIA) and several United States agencies carried out detailed intelligence studies and surveillance that were critical for the success of the operation. During the intelligence studies, the Americans properly located where Osama bin Laden was living, his security networks and strengths, and of course options on how to fly into Pakistan undetected by their military radar as well as on the best attack strategy once on the ground. The Pakistani's defensive capabilities were known since the US had helped equip and train the Pakistanis. The weather was studied to investigate prospective weather conditions for a raid operation (weather forecast showed little moonlight over the area which would create poor visibility and prevent the neighborhood from easily noticing the operation). With the promising little moonlight and the interruption of electricity supply to the neighborhood, perfect darkness over the area was created for a secret operation of this nature (The SEALs wore night vision goggles). Although I have barely scratched the surface in discussing the SEAL's Intelligence operations that led to the killing of Osama bin Laden, however, the success of this critical operation was hinged on a properly-carried out intelligence. As you can see, the SEALs, not only killed the enemy but also received an ice on the cake as there was no American casualty.

Intelligence failure is most likely to end up in serious casualties like the ones that happened to the Americans during the America-Vietnam War. I pause as I recall to mind countless Christians all over the world (in ages) who are simply wounded and defeated soldiers of Christ—with broken legs (spiritual lameness), broken hands (amputated destinies), bleeding hearts (broken hearts), and headless (living purposeless lives). For how long would this continue? It is an unfortunate situation that the Church has suffered many casualties and have lost many of her soldiers! I am afraid that there are more spiritual disabilities among Christians than there are physical disabilities in the world. God does not want to see His soldiers being beaten and crawling like millipedes in shame. It hurts God to see that! God wants to see the Church use the weapons of His all-surpassing power to wreck the world of darkness.

God has given His people heavenly weapons to fight the enemy because He knows that we are in the midst of wolves **(Matthew 10:16)** and that these *"savage wolves will come in...not sparing the flock"* **(Acts 20:29).** The weapons of our warfare that God has given to us *"are not carnal, but mighty through God to the pulling down of strongholds"* **(2 Corinthians 10:4).** It is through these spiritual weapons of warfare that we obtain victory from God as He fights the battle Himself. We have God's Word on that! God has provided for us His whole armor with which we shall fight the enemy **(Ephesians 6:10-17)**—and it is our responsibility to use such weapons of enormous power in spiritual engagements! We are the Lord's battle ax **(Jeremiah 51:20)!**

Understand that when you fight with God's weapons, you will win the battle all the time, provided that you know how to use the weapons effectively. God's people must, therefore, be skillful in the art of spiritual warfare operations, most especially engagements of intelligence and with the use of weapons of warfare. A good intelligence reveals the weaknesses of your enemy—and that is exactly where you should focus your prayer attacks.

The Bible provides us with all of the intelligence that we need to know about in regard to how the enemy functions. The Bible, in this sense, is the believer's manual that we should study in order to be equipped with tactical survival skills to deal with the kingdom of darkness. The Bible, itself, is a weapon of warfare! However, we need the Holy Spirit to tap into the Intelligence Headquarters of Heaven so that we can harness specific details of particular demonic spirits as well as God's plan on how to attack them.

At this point, I wish to make it clear—as we can see from the America-Vietnam War—that the winning army in a battle engagement usually possesses superior skills in the reconnaissance of the enemy forces, not necessarily (and not always) possessing superior forces or armament. Yes, the people of God possess the superior powers of Heavenly weapon but, we must gauge the strengths and weaknesses of the enemy that we have come to fight. This is important in spiritual warfare because it is a very serious battle in which there shall be casualties—and you don't want to be the one to suffer the casualties. The spiritual enemies that we have come to fight is tremendously armed against you! The devil will always work to wear down the saints with his attacks **(Daniel 7:25).** They have a super high spiritual artillery and networks of spiritual satellite control systems (demonic observers) that monitor the activities of the people of God. For instance, when you are under a high-gravity attack, you can be certain that the spiritual tyrants have their satellite system focused on you! We must chain the enemy with the weapon of our prayers. Do you see why a prayerless Christian can't even stand the enemy?

The saying that power is relative is true. Compared to God, the devil and his messengers or co-tyrants do not possess great power. However, compared to mankind in the flesh, the devil and his messengers are very powerful indeed. On this ground alone, we must have Christ in us and know how to fight spiritual wars with God's weapons—for only by this way shall we keep the enemy aloof. Without Jesus Christ in our lives, we would be like finely dressed soldiers without any weapons to confront our spiritual enemies. The enemy is not afraid of you because you claim to be a Christian, but because he knows that you know your authority in Christ and also know how to use your spiritual weapons. He is afraid when he knows that you are battle-ready to use your spiritual weapons against him! Do you see why a prayerless Christian is simply a powerless Christian?

The Children of God must wake up and realize that they are always at war—always, not sometimes! We ought to understand that we must use the weapons of Heaven and Spirit-inspired strategies to fight the adversary. Like the Vietnamese, we need a battle plan. We need specific tactics for specific skirmishes. Anything short of this is a colossal defeat. Hear me very well: whether you believe it or not, you are at war! So, would you make a resolution right now to walk on your authority as a Christian and then use it in spiritual warfare against the Kingdom of Darkness? If they can stop you now from making this decision, you will never mature to the point of being much of a threat to them in spiritual battles.

The weapons of our warfare against the spiritual tyrants are: The Blood of Jesus Christ, The Name of Jesus Christ, The Fire of God; The Word of God, Praise and the Confessions of our mouth, Fasting and Prayer, The Holy Eucharist, The Rosary, and many more that I do not have the luxury of space here to expound. [Please, see my books titled, *"The Warrior's Weapons"* for more revealing details on this subject]. Use these weapons, and the enemy cannot stand you in any spiritual battle!

Regrettably, many people of God have just passively slipped and spiraled downwards into a prayerless living. When will you decide to put on your spiritual armor and dress for spiritual battles? When will you decide to make heaven proud of you as you use those spiritual armors to fight the spiritual forces that are molesting your life? I don't think that you have any time left to make that decision. It has to be now! The gravity of the raging war calls for you to make that decision now. I can't help but think of the marketer who is mounting pressure on his client to buy a product saying, *"Put on the boot now and let me watch you march on the nails!"* So I tell you: **"Therefore put on the full armor of God"** (Ephesians 6:13, NIV), and with your threshing boot, let God see you **"thresh the mountains and crush them, and ... make the hills like chaff"** (Isaiah 41:15). Before we conclude this chapter, I will leave you with three things to do: (1) put off the cloak of prayerlessness now, (2) put on your full spiritual armor now, and then (3) put up for a fight with the devil now. Do them now! If you have done these, then you are ready to run through the enemy's troop with your artillery of God's weapons.

LET US PRAY!

1. Reflect on how this reflection on "Weapons Against the Spiritual Tyrants" ministers to you.

2. Pray the Saint Michael the Archangel prayer (see page 17).

3. Pray the Anima Christi prayer (see page 18)

4. Pray **Psalm 76** (a prayer for the victorious Power of God).

5. Jesus defeated the devil on the Cross. Taking the Cross as a weapon against the enemy, place yourself and your family now under the Cross of Jesus Christ. Pray the following, adding "in the name of Jesus Christ" at the end of every prayer point.
   a. The Body of Christ on the Cross takes all the bullets and arrows of Satan shot at me and my family;
   b. The Blood of the crucified Christ shields me and my family from every harm;
   c. I count upon the crucified Christ to shield me from above and beneath, on my right and my left, in front of me and behind me, that I might be protected, walled in, encapsulated in a way that Satan may never gain any access to hurt or destroy me from fulfilling my destiny.

6. Confess the following weapons of warfare as you engage in a spiritual battle. In the name of Jesus Christ, I confess:
   a. That I have conquered the demonic forces by the

Blood of Jesus Christ and by the word of my testimony **(Revelation 12:11)**;

b. That the Word of God is a spiritual two-edged sword in my hand piercing and cutting through the enemy **(Hebrews 4:12, Ephesians 6:17)**;

c. That the *"burning coals [that] went forth at His feet"* shall burn down to ashes every demonic altar that is speaking against me **(Habakkuk 3:5, KJV)**;

d. *"That at the name of Jesus every knee should bow, of those in heaven, and of those on earth, and of those under the earth"* **(Philippians 2:10, NKJV)**;

e. That where I am cast down by the enemy's blow, I am confessing that *"there is [a] lifting up"* **(Job 22:29, AKJV)**;

f. That as I praise God, all the prison doors shall be thrown open, and everyone's chains shall come loose **(Acts 16:26)**;

g. That my *"tongue is like a sharp razor"* **(Psalm 52:2)**, like *"sharp swords"* **(Psalm 57:4)**, like a "deadly arrow" **(Jeremiah 9:8)**, *"like bows"* **(Jeremiah 9:3)**, and even like a piercing two-edged knife **(Hebrews 4:12)**;

h. That with my mouth, I command every mountain: *"Be taken up and thrown into the sea"* **(Mark 11:23)**;

i. That every stubborn problem must go by my *"prayer and fasting"* **(Matthew 17:21, NASB)**;

j. That *"the Spirit of the Lord is upon me... to proclaim freedom for the prisoners and recovery of sight for the blind, to set the oppressed free"* **(Luke 4:18)**;

k. That *"the yoke shall be destroyed because of the anointing"* **(Isaiah 10:27)**;

l. That *"the angel of the Lord [is] driving them away"* **(Psalm 35:5)**;

m. That the Lord promises me in **Exodus 33:2** saying, *"I will send an angel before you, and I will drive out the"* enemies;

n. That I shall *"chase a thousand"* enemies **(Deuteronomy 32:30)**;

o. That through my faith in God, I have overcome the world (1 John 5:4);

p. That I am the Lord's *"battle-ax and weapons of war"* (Jeremiah 51:20) for with me, He shall break the enemies into pieces;

q. That the Spirit helps me in my weakness (Romans 8:26), *"for whenever I am weak, then I am strong"* (2 Corinthians 12:10);

r. That I have the mind of Christ (Philippians 2:5), and so the enemy cannot outwit me in this battle (2 Corinthians 2:11);

s. That the power of Christ from my altar of prayer shall seize and destroy every evil operation, and shall tear down and burn to ashes all evil altars (1 Kings 13:4-5);

t. That I have the authority to *"cast out demons"* in the name of Jesus Christ (Mark 16:17);

u. That the Lord Jesus Christ shall *"train me for battle, so that I can use the strongest bow"* as a weapon to fight the enemy (Psalm 18:34, GNT);

v. That the Lord Jesus Christ shall train *"my hands for war, and my fingers for battle"* (Psalm 144:1);

w. That in this battle, I am *"more than [a conqueror] through"* Christ (Romans 8:37) as I *"thresh the mountains and crush them, and ... make the hills like chaff"* (Isaiah 41:15);

x. That no weapon that is fashioned against me shall prosper (Isaiah 54:17);

y. That the Word of God in my mouth is a hammer with which I will shatter the plots of the devil against me (Jeremiah 23:29);

z. That I carry God's flames of fire (Hebrews 1:7), and—like Elijah in 2 Kings 1:9-15—I call down the fire of God to consume the bands of satanic hordes coming after me.

7. Thank the Lord and cover this prayer with the Most Precious Blood of Jesus Christ (7 times).

DAY 5

Part 2: Warfare Prayers

Note:

- The struggles we go through every day remind us that there is a spiritual conflict against the saints of God. We face a powerful enemy out to destroy us. We are at war! It's a spiritual war with crucial consequences in our everyday life and its outcome will determine our eternal destiny.

- God has given us spiritual weapons and armor to fight the enemy. We depend on the strength of God by fighting with His weapons and putting on His whole protective armor. Soldiers wear protective armor in order to fight well. No soldier would go into battle without his weapons and armor. If he did, he wouldn't live very long. Christians cannot survive in this spiritual war without fighting with the weapons and armor that God gave to them.

- We have to arm ourselves with the weapons of warfare that God has given to us. Are you ready for battle?

1. Lord Jesus, I worship You, and I give You praise. I recognize that You are worthy to receive all glory and honor and praise **(Revelation 4:11).**
   a. I surrender myself completely and unreservedly to the Holy Spirit to lead me into victory through this prayer;
   b. Holy Spirit help me to pray with depth and intensity;
   c. I cover myself and the environment of this prayer with the Most Precious Blood of our Lord Jesus Christ;
   d. Praise and worship God as the Holy Spirit leads you.

2. Pray **Psalm 51** and use it to prayerfully flow into asking God for the forgiveness of your sins. Therefore, in the name of Jesus Christ:

    a. I reject all the accusations of Satan against this prayer;

    b. I refuse to let sin have dominion over me.

3. Pray the prayer of Saint Michael the Archangel (see page 17).

4. Pray the Anima Christi prayer (see page 18).

5. I take a stand against all the workings of invisible spiritual forces that might plot to hinder me in this time of prayer.

6. I decree that my whole body is activated with fire for this warfare prayer against the Kingdom of darkness; in the name of Jesus Christ.

7. Lord Jesus Christ, I am thankful for the armor that You have provided for me in this prayer. Therefore, in the mighty name of Jesus Christ, I put on the full armor God **(Ephesians 6:13-17):**

    a. I put on the girdle of truth, the breastplate of righteousness, the sandals of peace, and the helmet of salvation;

    b. I lift up the shield of faith against all the fiery darts of the enemy, and take in my hand the sword of the spirit, the Word of God, and use the Word against all the forces of evil against my life;

    c. Lord, I lift up the shield of faith against all the blazing missiles that Satan and his hosts fire at me;

    d. I helmet my head with Jesus Christ.

8. The Word of God says in **Jeremiah 1:10,** *"See, today I appoint you over nations and over kingdoms, to pluck up and to pull down, to destroy and to overthrow, to build and to plant."* Therefore, in the name of Jesus Christ:

    a. I take authority over the kingdom of darkness;

    b. I uproot and pull down every satanic altar that is working against me;

    c. I destroy and overthrow every evil establishment that is against me.

9. In the name of Jesus Christ, I decree that:
    a. There will be no ground to give Satan a foothold against me again;
    b. All principalities and powers and all wicked spirits are subject to me;
    c. The weapons of my warfare are not carnal, but mighty through God to the pulling down of strongholds, to the casting down of imaginations and every high thing that exalts itself against the knowledge of God, and to bring every thought into obedience to the Lord Jesus Christ (**2 Corinthians 10:4**). Therefore, in the name of Jesus Christ:
        i. I tear down all demonic strongholds that are formed against me;
        ii. I cast down all satanic imaginations against me;
        iii. I pull down every high thing that exalts itself against the knowledge of God in this prayer and in my life;
        iv. I bring every thought into obedience to the Lord Jesus Christ.

10. Holy Spirit, enable me to uptain victory against the princes, powers, rulers, and wicked spirits who carry the battle of darkness against me, in the name of Jesus Christ.

11. Lord Jesus Christ, help me to keep my armor well-oiled with prayer, in the name of Jesus Christ.

12. I stand on **Job 5:19** to decree that the Lord shall deliver me *"from six troubles; in seven no harm shall touch"* me, in the name of Jesus Christ.

13. Ask the Holy Spirit to activate your spiritual eyes to see the hidden areas of your life that the devil holds hostage (and ask Him to also reveal to you the enemy's hiding places).
    a. Holy Spirit, show me areas of my life that the devil holds hostage;
    b. Holy Spirit, I ask that You reveal every enemy shooting

arrows at me from unknown sources—in the name of Jesus Christ.

c. Let all the invisible forces hiding in ..... (*pick from the following list*) be forced out of their hiding places—in the name of Jesus Christ.
- Rivers
- Air
- Ground
- Mountains
- Underground
- Human bodies
- Trees
- Animals
- Atmosphere

14. In the name of Jesus Christ (begin to declare aggressively as follows):
    a. I render all the weapons of the kingdom of darkness useless;
    b. I shall make ..... (*pick from the following list*) against the kingdom of darkness in this spiritual warfare—in the name of Jesus Christ.

    • A good offense   • A good defense   • An effective intelligence

15. I shall not be ..... (*pick from the following list*) by the enemies— in the name of Jesus Christ.
    - Outwitted
    - Understood
    - Disposed of
    - Defeated
    - Observed
    - Arrested
    - Tortured
    - Disadvantaged
    - Wounded
    - Disabled
    - Frustrated

16. I shall not suffer any casualty in this warfare prayers, in the name of Jesus Christ.

17. Thank You, Lord Jesus Christ, for answering my prayers and giving me victory.
    a. Sing songs of victory to the Lord;
    b. Offer thanksgiving prayers with **Psalm 117** and **Psalm 136.**

18. I cover this prayer with the Most Precious Blood of Jesus
    Christ (7 times).

Chapter 3

BRACE UP AGAINST THE TYRANTS

"You come to me with sword and spear and javelin; but I come to you in the name of the LORD of hosts, the God of the armies of Israel, whom you have defied. This very day the LORD will deliver you into my hand, and I will strike you down and cut off your head; and I will give the dead bodies of the Philistine army this very day to the birds of the air and to the wild animals of the earth, so that all the earth may know that there is a God in Israel, and that all this assembly may know that the LORD does not save by sword and spear; for the battle is the LORD's and he will give you into our hand."

(1 Samuel 17:45-47).

(Other suggested Bible passages to read:
2 Chronicles 20:1-29, 1 Samuel 17:1-58, Hebrews 11: 6-16,
Joshua 10:1-42, 1 Kings 18:1-45, Deuteronomy 31:6-7, Joshua 1:6-9).

DAY 6
Part 1: Reflection

Ships don't sink because of the water that is around them. Ships sink because of the water that gets into them. Ships go through storms as they sail in the ocean. To avoid sinking, they must brace up against the many storms that come their way as they carry their cargoes. History is full of destinies that got sunk in the sea of futility because the tyrants sneaked into their lives crippling their beauty and purpose. The tyrant spirits naturally bring wreck into people's lives. The tyrant will take hold of you and will make sure you lose all your possessions—finances, health, career, marriage, and passion. He has rendered many lives unproductive, stormy and catastrophic. The tyrant wants to take away everything that God has given to you. Do you still remember that it was when Babylon invaded Jerusalem and conquered the city that Jerusalem was razed down to the ground? She was forced, with her inhabitants, into exile in Babylon **(2 Chronicles 36:15-21)**. Jerusalem became a shadow of herself! Tyrants are like Babylon; they reduce life to misery. We have witnessed the decline of the very moral fabric of our nation itself because the spiritual tyrants, like the historical Babylon, are eating up the very values that we hold as a people of God.

On this backdrop, we find relief in the words of Charles Spurgeon: *"No saint shall fall finally or fatally. Sorrow may bring us to the earth, and death may bring us to the grave, but lower we cannot sink, and out of the lowest of all we shall arise to the highest of all."*

So, we have to brace up! Brace up yourself against the hostile wind that is sweeping from the desert and heading to your estate **(Job 1:19)**. Brace up when you find yourself stuck in the land of discouragement and the weeds of disappointment and bitterness are competing to take root in you. Brace up when in the midst of difficult circumstances. Brace up the next time any spiritual tyrant threatens to mire you down. Brace up the next time life's circumstances give you an excuse to blow out of the track and get stuck in the race. Brace up yourself, change is coming! Your tears would soon turn to laughter. The gloomy clouds would soon clear away. Don't you feel it in your spirit that the shackles are about to be broken? Brace up, my friend! You are a prayer away from your victory!! Again, I say: Brace up!!!

Brace up because the enemy wants you dead—*"Like a roaring lion, your adversary, the devil prowls around, looking for someone to devour"* (1 Peter 5:8). Brace up because God is with you—and that's all that you really need to have victory. In Joshua 10:1-42, we see a very bad situation in which Joshua and the children of Israel were facing the armies of five kings. In the natural, it seemed to be a hopeless war, but they took faith in God and braced up themselves against the enemies. The result was that the Lord fought for His people and defeated their enemies. So, likewise, the Lord will defeat the spiritual enemies of your life, if you ask Him to fight for you. Perhaps your heart is heavy. Perhaps, you may be grieving now for maybe over a thousand reasons: your depressed children, your unloving spouse, your dashed hopes, your deceased loved ones, or your ruinous sin—but the Lord says, *"Brace up, and give them to me."* Just do it, even if it doesn't make sense! Can you relate to wanting something so bad and wondering why God wasn't giving it to you too soon? Even at that, brace up!

I like what I see when I read Hebrews 11: 6-16—I see real people, living in a world like yours and mine, who braced up with faith in God, refusing to get stuck in the mud of the discouraging circumstances in which they found themselves. The common thread woven through these individuals is the fact that nothing could deter them from keeping their trust in God. They refused to get stuck in the muddy pit! They braced up against the threatening tides! God was so pleased with them that He was *"not ashamed to be called their God; indeed, He has prepared a city for them"* (Hebrews 11:16).

Could it be said of you that you truly set your faith in God to bring about the good you hope for, despite the troubles that the devil brings your way? My dear, whatever you face today, be encouraged by the exceptional faith of these heroes of faith who are presented to us in **Hebrews 11: 6-16.** You can go through the fire with your faith intact. As long as you are running in the right direction—to Jesus—you'll find the grace and strength you will need to forge ahead! Jesus promised He will be with us always **(Matthew 28:20)**—and He never breaks His promises! So, brace up!

If you are convinced that you are in the right standing with God, then brace yourself up for the Lord is on your side (seek the Lord in fasting and prayer)[1] You may have become weary with moaning, but God cannot become weary with listening to your supplications **(Psalm 6:6–9).**

He gathers up all your tears and puts them in His bottle—the Psalmist cried, *"Put my tears in your bottle"* (Psalm 56:8). Jesus kneels with the grieving and collects their tears. Like a mother sitting beside her child's sickbed, God marks every sigh of discomfort and pain we go through. Your anguish may have gone unnoticed by others, but not one moment has it escaped the attention of God. Do you hear Him saying to you *"I have heard your prayer, I have seen your tears; indeed, I will heal you"* **(2 Kings 20:5).**

Every tear you shed in faith sinks down into the ground like a seed, waiting to sprout up into an oak of laughter. Be reminded that not one sparrow falls to the ground without God's notice **(Matthew 10:29),** and neither does one of your tears. The

---

1. If you haven't fully given your life to God, then genuine repentance and honest renunciation of habitual sin are very critical for your victory. Dedicate your life to Jesus Christ.

God who saw the misery of His people in Egypt **(Exodus 3:7)** and came *"down to deliver them from the Egyptians"* **(Exodus 3:8)** will not reproach you for the tears you shed as you walk through the ruins of this broken world. Every drop of tear offered to God has an invisible word of hope in it saying, *"The Lord is near to the brokenhearted"* **(Psalm 34:18)**. Every tear you offer to God is preparing for you *"an eternal weight of glory beyond all comparison"* **(2 Corinthians 4:17)**—and one day, with your cracked and weary voice, you shall praise Him saying, *"You have delivered my soul from death, my eyes from tears, my feet from stumbling; I will walk before the Lord in the land of the living"* **(Psalm 116:8-9)**. So, brace up!

Yes, it is true that the devil is an expert in carrying out warfare against God's people, but God says He wants you to brace up so as to be used to save this sin-sick, crying, desolate, and dying world. The ability to wage successful spiritual warfare against the satanic kingdom is very important for a bountiful and effective harvest of souls in this end time.

Our salvation rests on God's unchanging character to deliver His people who trust in Him. We need to understand that we're in a battle and there's a competing agenda. Spiritual warfare, the likes of which we've never witnessed, rages on. It is intense today and the conflict will only intensify and grow worse until the Lord returns. We witness increased attacks, both in frequency and severity—don't we? For sure, the power of the devil would become very great in the last days. We used to smell the enemy in the air, but now we see him sitting unchallenged before our eyes—in the media, in the Government, and even in the Church! He spews his torrential flood to sweep people away **(Revelation 12:15)**. He wants your name listed among the casualties of the spiritual war. He has made the used-to-be peaceful world to become a dangerous place to live in. He works hard to control everyone and doesn't want people to walk away from him. He wants to be causing heartbreaking experiences, imprisonment, and the feeling of disappointment in your God who promises you freedom. He creates problems for every true Christian today.

Yet, as soldiers of Christ, a retreat is not an option—neither is whining or freaking out. We have to brace up against the devil, *for by resisting the devil, he will flee from us* (James 4:7). We have to face the spiritual tyrants and engage them in warfare. Let the tyrants feel the crescendo of hammer blows from your prayers. Brace up, child of God! The Word of God assures us in **Romans 8:37** that *"In all these things we are more than conquerors through him who loved us."* That does not mean we will not suffer attacks—remember that this is a war! Attacks are inevitable components of wars. In fact, if we are not being attacked, we should be concerned with whether or not we are really the soldiers of Christ.

We need to brace up like David to confront the Goliaths that are warring against us. God, through His covenant, has equipped the Church to confront and subvert the enemies. Regrettably, many people of God do not walk in their covenant relationship with God—thereby walking defeated, never raising up their heads. Every man in Israel was in covenant with God but only David walked in the covenant as he braced himself up against Goliath in a fight. With every odd against David—no protective military wear, no spear, no sword, and being inexperienced—he came to the war field with his covenant with God.

In spiritual warfare, it is your covenant that fights for you! On the other hand, the Philistines have a covenant with their gods too, and that was why Goliath *"cursed David by his gods"* (**1 Samuel 17:43**)—meaning that their gods would fight David.

David anchored on his covenant with God, and so did Goliath on his gods. Actually, this was a war of God versus gods! This was a war between two different and opposite set of invisible forces!

Put yourself in the shoes of David. He did not have the Bible to read the outcome with Goliath beforehand—as we do today. Imagine a giant of the caliber described in 1 **Samuel 17:4-7** charging against a small boy! Yet David had to trust in his covenant with God. He had faith that his God is faithful to deliver him based on the covenant. We have similar problems and trials today—don't we? Following the footsteps of David, we shall overcome every tyrant as we brace ourselves up, appropriating our covenant relationship with God. God is still searching for someone, like David, who would brace up against the tyrants and declare his covenant sacred anthem (1 **Samuel 17:45-47**):

> *"You come to me with sword and spear and javelin; but I come to you in the name of the LORD of hosts, the God of the armies of Israel, whom you have defied. This very day the LORD will deliver you into my hand, and I will strike you down and cut off your head; and I will give the dead bodies of the Philistine army this very day to the birds of the air and to the wild animals of the earth, so that all the earth may know that there is a God in Israel, and that all this assembly may know that the LORD does not save by sword and spear; for the battle is the LORD's and he will give you into our hand."*

The above Scripture is an eloquent testimony of David's unshakable confidence in God. He braced up himself against the giant and became the killer of the killer. Behind the curtain, David has been spending time with God and came to develop a relationship of trust in His faithfulness to save him in the time of trouble. Investing time in prayer enhances our relationship with God too, and builds our astuteness to brace up with courage when the tyrants emerge. Therefore, *"be strong and bold; have no fear or dread of them, because it is the LORD your God who goes with you; he will not fail you or forsake you"* (Deuteronomy 31:6).

LET US PRAY!

1. Reflect on how this reflection on "Brace Up Against the Tyrants" ministers to you.

2. Pray the Saint Michael the Archangel prayer (see page 17).

3. Pray the Anima Christi prayer (see page 18).

4. Pray **Psalm 17** for God's deliverance from affliction.

5. The Lord who in **Joshua 10:1-42** delivered His people from a seemingly hopeless war shall see me through all that I am going through now—in the name of Jesus Christ.

6. In the name of Jesus Christ, I refuse to sink in life. Use the name of Jesus Christ after each of the following declarations:
   a. I decree that every package of the enemy to sink me is aborted;
   b. What is projected to sink me shall not come near me;
   c. What is projected to sink me shall not enter into me;
   d. No storms that I go through in life shall sink me;

e. My life cannot be wrecked, no matter what I go through!

f. Like Noah's ark, I shall sail on the flood that is sent to drown me;

g. I shall brace up against every storm that comes against me;

h. I shall walk victoriously through the ruins of this broken world;

i. I shall not be crippled nor be trapped in the sea of futility;

j. I reject unproductive, stormy, and catastrophic life;

k. I refuse to become a shadow of myself!

l. I shall not fall fatally—and even if I fall, I shall rise again to the topmost;

m. I command every hostile wind that is targeting me and my family to backfire;

n. I shall walk in my covenant relationship with God;

o. I am winning this war because I find the grace and strength I need in Jesus Christ.

7. The Word of God assures me in **Romans 8:37** that *"In all these things we are more than conquerors through him who loved us."* Therefore, in the name of Jesus Christ...

a. My name shall not be listed under the list of the casualties of spiritual war;

b. I take a stand in this prayer to resist the devil, and he must flee from me **(James 4:7)**.

8. Thank the Lord and cover this prayer with the Most Precious Blood of Jesus Christ (7 times).

DAY 7

Part 2: Warfare Prayers

Note:

- If you haven't fully given your life to God, then genuine repentance and honest renunciation of habitual sin are very critical for your victory in this prayer. Dedicate your life to Jesus Christ.

- If you have some specific issues in your life, then mention them as you pray this prayer.

- Seek the Lord with fasting and prayer.

1. Offer Praise to God:
   a. Praise God with **Psalm 118:28-29**—*"You are my God, and I will praise You; You are my God, I will exalt You. Oh, give thanks to the Lord, for He is good! For His mercy endures forever"* (NKJV);
   b. Praise God with **Psalm 145:3-4** (NKJV)—*"Great is the Lord, and greatly to be praised; and His greatness is unsearchable. One generation shall praise Your works to another, and shall declare Your mighty acts"*;
   c. Offer God Spirit-filled praise and worship songs as the Spirit leads.

2. Make a prayer of plea for God's mercy with **Psalm 51**. Confess your sins to God.
   a. *Lord, have mercy on me, a sinner;*
   b. Ask the Holy Spirit to help you locate anything that might be giving the devil a doorway into your life... and ask Him to help you deal with it.;
   c. Renounce all covenants, curses, agreements and all unholy alliances of the past.

3. Pray the prayer of Saint Michael the Archangel (see page 17).

4. Pray the Anima Christi prayer (see page 18).

5. Lord Jesus Christ, give me the courage to stand against the enemy in the course of this prayer, in the name of Jesus.
   a. I put on the armor of God: the helmet of salvation, the breastplate of righteousness, the belt of truth, the sandals of the gospel of peace, the sword of the Spirit, which is the Word of God, and the shield of faith **(Ephesians 6:13-17)**.
   b. Thank You Lord Jesus, for your promise that greater is He that is in me than He that is in the world **(1 John 4:4)**.

6. O Lord Jesus, come and fight this battle for me—I ask in the name of Jesus Christ.

7. Anchor on your covenant with God...and begin to pray (use the name of Jesus Christ after each prayer).
   a. As David's covenant with God brought him victory over Goliath, so shall my covenant with God bring victory my way through this prayer—in the name of Jesus Christ;
   b. As Goliath *"cursed David by his gods"* and it had no effect **(1 Samuel 17:43)**—so by reason of my covenant with God, shall every curse that was spoken against me not have any effect on me.

8. Declare your covenant sacred anthem with David **(1 Samuel 17:45-47)**. Pray this anthem with seriousness:

   "You come to me with sword and spear and javelin;
   but I come to you in the name of the LORD of hosts,
   the God of the armies of Israel, whom you have defied.
   This very day the LORD will deliver you into my
   hand, and I will strike you down and cut off your

head; and I will give the dead bodies of the Philistine army this very day to the birds of the air and to the wild animals of the earth, so that all the earth may know that there is a God in Israel, and that all this assembly may know that the LORD does not save by sword and spear; for the battle is the LORD's and he will give you into our hand."

9. In the name of Jesus Christ, my----- (*pick from the following list*) shall not sink, and even if it has gotten sunk, it must be rescued today.
   - Destiny
   - Joy
   - Business
   - Health
   - Glory & beauty
   - Prayer life
   - Possessions
   - Testimonies
   - Family
   - Miracles
   - Career
   - Victory
   - Marriage
   - Blessings
   - Profits
   - Finances

10. Begin to make the following confession (use the name of Jesus Christ after each of the following declarations):
    a. I confess that the shackles over me are getting to be broken now!
    b. I confess with my mouth that positive change is coming my way!
    c. I confess that my tears will soon turn to laughter!
    d. I confess that my victory is now!

11. In the name of Jesus Christ, I brace up myself against every arrow of ----- (*pick from the following list*) that is targeting my life and family.
    - Death
    - Misery
    - Discouragement
    - Threats
    - Tears
    - Grief & anguish
    - Gloomy clouds
    - Abandonment
    - Sickness
    - Broken heartedness
    - Disappointment

- Difficulty
- Very bad situations
- Terrible sword
- Storm & oppression
- Constant Failure
- Hopelessness
- Calamity
- Bitterness
- Defeat
- Shame
- Dashed hopes
- Poverty
- Disfavor

12. Despite the troubles that the devil brings my way, I continue to set my faith in God to bring about the good I hope for—in the name of Jesus Christ.

13. Lord Jesus Christ, Your Word says in **Matthew 7:7** to ask and I shall receive. Therefore, in the name of Jesus Christ, I ask...
    a. For the exceptional faith of those heroes in **Hebrews 11: 6-16;**
    b. For the grace to have an unshakable faith in God;
    c. For the grace to keep running to Jesus Christ.

14. I decree that every tear that I shed is a seed that shall soon sprout up into an oak of laughter.

15. *"If you do not stand firm in faith, you shall not stand at all"* **(Isaiah 7:9b)**. Therefore, I stand firm in faith and decree that when I am ----- (*pick from the following list*) I shall brace up against the enemy, in the name of Jesus Christ.

    - In sorrow
    - Forsaken
    - Mourning
    - Desolate
    - Abandoned
    - Surrounded by anguish
    - Surrounded by the sea of bitterness
    - Overwhelmed by grief
    - In the field of tribulation
    - Weak, wrecked & wretched
    - Afflicted
    - In tears
    - Heartbroken
    - In desolation
    - Troubled

16. O Lord Jesus, visit me and destroy every work of the enemy against me—I pray in the name of Jesus Christ.

17. Now, brace up in prayer using the following Scriptures to gain victory over the invisible forces that are fighting you. Make the following prayers *in the name of Jesus Christ*:

   a. **"Let all those be put to shame and confusion who seek to snatch away my life; let those be turned back and brought to dishonor who desire my hurt"** (Psalm 40:14).

      i. *May all who want to take my life be put to shame and confusion; may all who desire my ruin be turned back in disgrace;*

      ii. *Confuse them! Turn them around all those who are trying to destroy me. Disgrace these scoffers with their utter failure!*

      iii. **"Let them be turned back and brought to confusion that devise my hurt"** (Psalm 35:4, KJV) ;

      iv. Lord Jesus, frustrate the mission of *those* **who are trying to kill me**. *Turn them back and confuse them in Jesus name.*

   b. **"Let their lying lips be silenced"** (Psalm 31:18);

   c. The wicked shall stumble and perish at God's Presence **(Psalm 9:3)**;

   d. **"Let not mine enemies triumph over me"** (Psalm 25:2, KJV);

   e. I stand on **Isaiah 54:17** to decree that no weapon that is formed against me shall prosper, and every tongue that rises against me in judgment shall be condemned, in Jesus Christ's name.

18. Holy Spirit, grant that I brace up with more fire in me, no matter the troubles I go through in life, in the name of Jesus Christ.

19. Lord Jesus Christ, I hear You in **2 Kings 20:5** telling me: *"I have heard your prayer, I have seen your tears; indeed, I will heal you."* I believe Your Word, and I know You have heard and answered my prayers.

   a. I shall praise You, Lord Jesus, for *"You have delivered my soul from death, my eyes from tears, my feet from stumbling; I will walk before the Lord in the land of the living"* (Psalm 116:8-9);

b. Thank You, Lord Jesus Christ, for giving me the grace to brace up against the invisible enemies that are fighting my destiny.

   i. Sing songs of victory to the Lord;

   ii. Offer thanksgiving prayers with **Psalm 29** and **Psalm 104.**

20. I cover this prayer with the Most Precious Blood of Jesus Christ (7 times).

Chapter 4

NEVER SURRENDER!

· · ◆ ◆ ◆ ◆ ◆ · ·

"But you, take courage! Do not let your hands be weak, for your work shall be rewarded."

2 Chronicles 15:7

"Do not fear, for I am with you, do not be afraid, for I am your God; I will strengthen you, I will help you, I will uphold you with my victorious right hand."

Isaiah 41:10

(Other suggested Bible passages to read:
Isaiah 40:29-31, Joshua 1:9, Hebrews 12:1-3, Philippians 4:13,
2 Corinthians 4:8-11, Psalm 37:24, Galatians 6:9).

DAY 8

Part 1: Reflection

Think of a seed. You bury it in the ground. You throw dirt at it. Beneath the dead leaves and decomposing plants of the previous season, the seed lies. Sometimes, it is buried underneath the snow and ice. Storm comes. Rain comes. The sun heats. Yet, it always grows back to life! It bursts forth with life. It even grows back stronger, bigger, and more beautiful than ever! A seed never surrenders its destiny! The world throws mud at it but it never surrenders. Through the darkness of the deep soils, it rises to show the world its beauty. Through the storms, it emerges with the strength of unsurrendering purpose and optimism. In the midst of dead leaves and rotten plants, it never feels dead inside but it rather finds reasons to see life. It hopes for life and so it finds life. I hear the seed saying, *"You can't bury me! I cannot surrender to my enemies!"*

You see, one may try to bury power or passion, but it won't stay buried. You can't bury the purpose of a man strongly motivated to survive. One may try to bury fire, but that is not possible because fire has power. Prophet Jeremiah tried to shut up the Word of God (which is fire) in him but he couldn't as it became **"something like a burning fire shut up in [his] bones" (Jeremiah 20:9)**. Fire breaks the bottle that tries to conceal it, just as the seed breaks the soil that tries to bury it. Similarly, one may try to bury love, but it cannot be contained. **Song of Solomon 8:7** says that **"Many waters cannot quench love, neither can floods drown it."**

The character of the seed is the spirit that God wants to see in us. The seed never surrenders. So too God does not want us to surrender our destinies to the enemy. Life may throw dirt or storms at us or throw us into life's trash cans, or—like a sardine—bury us in the valley of dry bones or entrap us in the midst of Death Valley; yet, God is able to bring us to life again. We miss the mark when we feel dead inside. Nothing can compensate for a life that has surrendered to the enemy. We should not surrender to whatever the enemy throws at us. In Him is everything we shall ever need to be successful in overcoming the challenges we go through **(2 Peter 1:3)**. We are indomitable in Christ!

Now, let's talk. Supposing a man approaches you with a dagger and you know without an iota of doubt that he has only one thing in his mind to do—and that is to kill you. Would you surrender to him or would you use every breath in you to fight for your life? I believe your attitude in the fight would be to save your life by all means. Isn't it? That is the unsurrendering attitude of the seed. It fights to survive! Your attitude to the danger of being confronted by a killer would not be different if such an enemy is coming to attack you with an agenda to kill you. For sure, the knowledge of a man's avid desire to kill you provokes you to fight to overpower the enemy—and you have no apology to make for showing no mercy to the enemy in fighting him to save your life. The same is true concerning our conflict with the devil and his tyrants. They have no mercy in reserve for you at all. In fact, they come to kill and destroy (John 10:10). Therefore, we should fight them back with no mercy. The devil and his allied tyrants have attacked us a long time with fierceness in an effort to destroy our assignments on earth. We should fight the devil harder: NO RETREAT, NO SURRENDER!

I wish to tell you a short story. It is a story that encourages us never to surrender. It was in early June of 1940. The World War had broken out and every odd was against Great Britain. Adolf Hitler, an infamous historical tyrant had threatened to attack Britain. France has surrendered to Hitler's army. Hitler then assumed that Britain would simply surrender to him, having defeated France. It was in the face of this bleak dilemma that the British Prime Minister, Winston Churchill, rose to address his people:

> *"We are told that . . . Hitler has a plan for invading the British Isles. . . . We shall fight on the beaches, we shall fight on the landing grounds, we shall fight in the fields and in the streets, we shall fight in the hills; we shall never surrender."*

I believe that Winston Churchill's message to his British soldiers is a piece of fitting advice to the good soldiers of Christ in the battlefields of life. We should not surrender our destinies to the enemy. We shall fight with the determination of David until the tyrant is downed and decapitated. David silenced Goliath by taking a fight against him. You cannot silence the spiritual tyrants in your life until you are ready to engage them in a fierce fight. You must not surrender, my friend! Here, the advice of Richard Nixon is well-fitting: "A man is not finished when he is defeated. He is finished when he quits the fight."

When we surrender, we give up the very fight that keeps our testimonies. How can you resist the devil when you surrender to him **(James 4:7)**? To surrender is to accept the devil's verdict over your situation. We cannot expect light at the end of the tunnel when we surrender to the enemies. Do not let your present circumstances dictate the way forward. Surrendered folks are captured people. There are many battles in a war: you may lose a battle, but don't surrender to the war! Most people give up when they are just moments away from their long-awaited breakthroughs.

The Bible is full of people who refused to surrender to their enemies: The lepers in Samaria did not surrender to the debilitating situation they found themselves during the great famine **(2 Kings 7:3-8)**, and neither did the blind Bartimaeus surrender to his disability **(Mark 10:46-52)**. Hannah did not surrender to barrenness **(1 Samuel 1:19-20)** and neither did Sarah and Abraham **(Romans 4:16-21)**. David refused to surrender to King Saul's aggressive attempts to kill him **(1 Samuel 19-24)**. Daniel refused to surrender to the decree not to pray **(Daniel 6:22)**. Shadrach, Meshach, and Abednego refused to surrender to the decree to bow down to an idol **(Daniel 3:16)**, and Nehemiah never surrendered to the constant insults from Sanballat, Tobiah, and Geshem when he was building the broken walls of Jerusalem **(Nehemiah 2:19)**. Joseph rose from prison to the palace, never surrendering his destiny to the situations that he was going through **(Genesis 37:23-36)**. Mordecai refused to surrender to Haman's plot to kill him **(Esther 3:5-15)**. Queen Esther refused to surrender in saving her people **(Esther 5-10)**. Space may not allow me to detail the unsurrendering faith of the first century Church in spite of the severe persecution. We have a list of heroes of our faith in **Hebrews 11:33-35** who conquered the enemy simply because they refused to surrender.

In all of these Biblical references, *"the Lord rescues them"* from the *"many afflictions of the righteous"* **(Psalm 34:19)**. Why do you think that He will change now in your own situation? Always remember that the mighty God living in you is greater than he that is in the world **(1 John 4:4)**. God promises never to leave you nor forsake you **(Hebrew 13:5)**. Listen: instead of surrendering to your enemy, rather surrender your life and the situation that you are going through to the living God. We have new vitality and strength when we hand things over to God. Show me an unsurrendering child of God, and I will show you someone who never gives up, never gives in, never stops, and never quits the fight! Is your bell ringing: "No Retreat! No Surrender! No quitting!"

As I am writing the prayer points section of this chapter, I perceive in my spirit to go back to tell somebody whose bell is ringing "No Surrender" that Jesus is praying for you that your faith does not fail, though the enemy desires to sift you like wheat **(Luke 22:32)**. Could it be that, it is because of you that the Lord asked me to go back here to put this paragraph down just to tell you that He is standing in the gap for you over the situation that you are going through? Believe it because He says so! He cannot lie. Don't forget that *"He is able to save completely those who come to God through him, because he always lives to intercede for them"* **(Hebrews 7:25)**.

The primary reason why the devil sends tribulation or problems our way is to keep our mind away from God. If you are being overwhelmed with problems yourself, then make a decision right now to discipline yourself to fervently pray no matter what's going on. Prayer is a powerful weapon for those who have sworn never to surrender to the enemy's demands. This is one of the greatest weapons that we have against the kingdom of darkness.

Perhaps, the advice of Isaac to Esau is as well applicable to you: *"You will serve your brother. But when you grow restless, you will throw his yoke from off your neck"* (Genesis 27:40, NIV). To "grow restless" means to find it hard to sit still and allow things to go on as usual. It means that you are very uneasy with the situation that you are going through and that you are getting impatient, and are ready to cause trouble if you are delayed from taking action. Nothing can pacify a man who has come to the point of restlessness unless you allow him to have his way. Else, he will fight for his freedom. Could it be that God is telling you today what Isaac told Esau: *"You will be your tyrant's slave, but when you decide to take it no more and take up a fight with him, then you will break free from his tyranny"?* (Genesis 27:40, my translation).

This is to say that Esau must have the restlessness of a fighter before the yoke of Jacob on his neck shall be broken. He must be unsurrendering to the demands of Jacob. The way to move forward when a tyrant is standing on your way is to fight him. Do you envision a life free from tyrants? Don't wish it. Pray for it! Pray until you are free from the yoke of the tyrant. Don't allow your enemy to write the last chapter of your life. Are you tired of being oppressed or crushed by the spiritual tyrants? Prevail in prayer. Do you want to deliver your children from the mouth of the tyrants? Travail in the labor of prayer until Jesus Christ is formed in them (Galatians 4:19). Don't surrender!

Again, I say: "Don't surrender!" God looks at you and sees someone that is more than a conqueror in Christ **(Romans 8:37).** Conquerors don't surrender, you know! Rather, conquerors are vanquishers, not quitters. Do you still remember that after God created man, He blessed them, and said to them, *"Be fruitful and multiply, and fill the earth and subdue it; and have dominion over [it]"* **(Genesis 1:28).** God wants to see you walking in dominion, subduing every demand to stop you! He has put in you all that you needed to live as a conqueror. God didn't create you to be a victim. Rather, God created you to be a conqueror! In fact, everything that God created has built into it, its own success. For this reason, every seed buried in a moist ground grows. You will never see a bird that will not fly naturally, and you will never see a fish that won't swim naturally. God has put that nature or character in what He created for their success—but for a man, He built into him everything he needed to be in charge: subduing but not surrendering. God did not create failures! God created man to be successful. There's a crown that God has for only those who endured to the end, refusing to surrender to the demands of the devil—they shall wear the crown of life. What a motivation to keep fighting the good fight of faith **(1 Timothy 6:12).**

We offend the kingdom of darkness and cause havoc in their strongholds with our prayers when we decide to fight them— and not to surrender to them. They also fight back, and in most cases, our troubles may seem to be on the increase. But we should not allow the seemingly worsening situation to have our driver's seat. Remember that in **Revelation 12:7** when war broke out in heaven and St. Michael the Archangel and his angels fought against the dragon, the dragon and his angels also fought back. However St. Michael persevered in the fight until the enemy was routed out of Heaven. Heaven did not surrender to the enemy. Spiritual warfare, the likes of which we've never witnessed, rages on but with perseverance in prayer, we shall wear out the enemy.

So we should wrestle the enemy in prayer with unsurrendering spirit. Although the blessings of God are not obtained through our struggles but by His grace, yet it was not until Jacob took an all-night prayer-wrestling with God that his blessings really became his **(Genesis 32:22-32)**. Jacob's unrelenting struggles with God teaches us perseverance in prayer. Could God be using this event to train Jacob on the art of spiritual battle? I do know that God has to train His troops for war against the enemy. The Psalmist says, *"Blessed be the Lord my Rock and my great strength, who trains my hands for war and my fingers for battle"* **(Psalm144:1)**. David had to fight the lion and the bear before his historical fight with Goliath. Have you ever heard of an Army General who got his ranks without a war? In likewise a true soldier of Christ would have to fight many wars on his knees. Don't fear to fight those tough situations with your prayer! Call on the name of Jesus Christ to save you from the claws of that deadly tyrant. Like Samson, you can shut their mouths! Always remember that only in Christ shall we have our victory.

Before we conclude this reflection, I want to leave you with a word of hope that you can always count on when the devil is pressing hard to make you surrender to him— *"God keeps His promise [to deliver you]. He will not let you be tested beyond your strength. Along with the test, He will give you a way out of it so that you may be able to endure it"* **(1 Corinthians 10:13**, *my translation*). No temptation is new or peculiar to you. Do you hear God's soothing voice assuring you that although *"Many are the afflictions of the righteous, but the Lord rescues them from them all"* **(Psalm 34:19)**. So, God has already won the victory for us in Christ **(1 Corinthians 15:57-58)**!

We ought to anchor on Jesus' mighty strength and rely on His victory for us. Even if we walk on the path of trials, we should not gaze into the abyss of despair. We can be strong and always unrelenting because our strength is found in the strongest Warrior of all ages— Jesus Christ. The question for us at this moment is: "shall we surrender or shall we stand?" It is lamentable that many of the Lord's Generals who reigned yesterday in prayer as invincible fighters are, today, painfully ranked among the fallen Generals. History tells us that the Spartans are powerful warriors. Death for the Spartans was better than surrender! The lesson here is that we shouldn't surrender to the enemy, no matter the pressure! We need courage in the face of difficulties and trials. Think about this:

> "Whatever you do, you need courage. Whatever you decide upon, there is always someone to tell you, you are wrong. There are always difficulties arising which tempt you to believe that your critics are right. To map out a course of action, and follow it to the end, requires some of the same courage which a soldier needs. Peace has its victories, but it takes brave men to win them."—**Ralph Waldo Emerson.**

Yes, he is right: "It takes brave men to win" any battle. It took bravery for Apostle Paul to snap the viper into the fire that he set burning (**Acts 28:2-5**). Like Apostle Paul setting the fire that killed the viper, let your prayer carry the fire that will set the tyrant's camp on fire!

LET US PRAY!

I. Reflect on how this reflection on "Never Surrender" ministers to you.
   a. Have you surrendered to the enemy or been overcome by guilt? What are those ways (ask the Holy Spirit to help you bring them to mind)? Ask God to forgive you for the ways you have surrendered to the enemy's punch;
   b. Never surrender! Ask God to help you never to surrender to the enemy's fight but to face him squarely with prayers.

2. Pray the Saint Michael the Archangel prayer (see page 17).

3. Pray the Anima Christi prayer (see page 18).

4. Pray **Psalm 54** for God's deliverance from the enemy.

5. According to the provisions of **Isaiah 54:15,** I decree that anyone who attacks me shall surrender to me—I pray in the name of Jesus Christ.

6. Declare it loud and clear: "Devil, you can't bury me! I won't surrender to you, in the name of Jesus Christ!" Continue to declare the following using the "name of Jesus Christ" in each prayer point:
   a. I refuse to be another dry bone trapped in the valley of death;
   b. I refuse to feel dead inside of me;
   c. I refuse to be overpowered by the enemy;
   d. I refuse to accept the devil's final verdict over my situation;
   e. I must complete my assignments on earth;
   f. My faith in Jesus Christ shall lead me to victory;
   g. I will not let my present situation dictate the way to go;
   h. I refuse to be a captured soldier of Christ;
   i. I remain in prayer until I am free from the yoke of the tyrant;
   j. I throw the yoke of bondage off my neck **(Genesis 27:40)**;
   k. I must trouble satanic strongholds until victory is mine;
   l. I must see light at the end of the tunnel;
   m. I shall have a victory song at last;
   n. Begin to confess: "In the name of Jesus Christ, I am.....(*pick from the following list*), no matter what the devil does."

• Unstoppable	• Undeniable	• Unkillable
• Unaccusable	• Uncursable	• Uncrushable
• Untouchable	• Unarrestable	• Unconquerable
• Unbeatable	• Unsinkable	• Indomitable

7. According to **James 4:7**, I will resist the devil with my faith until he surrenders to me, in the name of Jesus Christ. Add "in the name of Jesus Christ" after each of the following prayers:
   a. I refuse to be numbered among the fallen Generals of the Lord's Army;
   b. According to **Hebrews 11:33-35**, I decree that I will:
      i. Subdue kingdoms like David;
      ii. Obtain God's promises for my life like Abraham;
      iii. Stop the mouths of lions like Daniel;
      iv. Quench the violence of the fire like Shadrack, Meshack, and Abednego;
      v. Restore the dead back to life again.
   c. I shall escape the chains and imprisonment of the enemy like Paul and Silas **(Acts 16:19-40)**;
   d. I shall escape the edge of the sword like Peter **(Acts 12:3-19)**;
   e. I shall become valiant in battle like Shamgar **(Judges 3:31)**;
   f. I shall turn to fight the armies of the aliens like David **(2 Samuel 22:38)**;
   g. I shall tread upon serpents and scorpions **(Luke 10:19)**.

8. Thank the Lord and cover this prayer with the Most Precious Blood of Jesus Christ (7 times).

DAY 9

Part 2: Warfare Prayers

Note:
- When soldiers are backed into a corner during a battle, they have two options: (1) To surrender, or (2) Never to

surrender. They can give up or they can face their enemy squarely. The gap between "surrender" and "never surrender" is a heightened tension between the two enemies. Don't allow your enemy to push you to surrender! You have to decide to defeat the enemy.

- Good soldiers of Christ never give in because Jesus Christ never gives up. With praise and worship songs, invite the Holy Spirit into this prayer to take charge.

1. Pray **Psalm 51** for the forgiveness of your sins.
    a. Forgive me Lord for the times I have surrendered to the enemy instead of trustingly surrendering to Your authority.
        i. I now surrender all to you (ask the Holy Spirit to reveal areas of your life that you have not fully surrendered to God);
        ii. Begin to surrender the situation to Him.
    b. I now surrender my will, thoughts, attitudes, and the longing of my heart, my disappointments, discouragements, and even all my despair to You Lord Jesus Christ.

2. The Psalmist says, *"Blessed be the Lord my Rock and my great strength, who trains my hands for war and my fingers for battle"* (Psalm144:1).
    a. Ask God to empower you in this spiritual battle;
    b. Ask Him to make you a dangerous fire that the devil cannot resist;
    c. I confess that only in Christ shall we have our victory.

3. Pray the prayer of Saint Michael the Archangel (see page 17).

4. Pray the Anima Christi prayer (see page 18).

5. Holy Spirit, with the oil of grace of **Zechariah 4:12,** anoint my heart and my mouth to pray my way to breakthrough through this prayer. In the name of Jesus Christ, I ask the Holy Spirit to:
   a. Lead me in this prayer, relying wholly on You;
   b. Help me to grow in grace with an attitude of fervent prayer without ceasing;
   c. Empower me to wrestle in prayer until God's will is done;
   d. Send His dew of glory over me in this prayer, and destroy the dew of Satan;
   e. Help me not to be afraid of the battle against evil.

6. Father, I know the battle belongs to You **(1 Samuel 17:47).** I also know You want me on the battlefield. Pray the following in the name of Jesus Christ:
   a. Help me to fight in the spirit, not in the flesh;
   b. May I never fight against people but against the kingdom of darkness **(Ephesians 6:12);**
   c. I claim Your promise to me saying, *"Fear not, I will help you"* **(Isaiah 41:13).**

7. Lord, grant that my prayer shall carry the fire that sets the tyrant's camp on fire—in the name of Jesus Christ.

8. Lord Jesus Christ, give me the strength to cling to Your promises when the world around me begins to shake or crumble— I pray in the name of Jesus Christ.

9. Lord Jesus Christ, You are the only foundation that can hold me up when the spiritual tyrants threaten me with trials and disaster. Pray the following in the name of Jesus Christ;
   a. Give me the strength of character I need to prove my faith in You;
   b. O Lord Jesus, give us sufficient grace, strength, and wisdom to face any trial and to answer any challenge to our faith.

10. *"The Lord will rescue me from every evil attack and save me for his heavenly kingdom"* (2 Timothy 4:18).

11. The Lord shall rescue me from the many afflictions that I am going through now **(Psalm 34:19)**—in the name of Jesus Christ.

12. I decree that whatever the enemies devised against me shall go back against them—in the name of Jesus Christ.

13. I decree that I will not retreat and I will not surrender to the enemy's pressure to make me quit—in the name of Jesus Christ!
    a. I will never surrender my destiny, in the name of Jesus Christ;
    b. Lord Jesus, like Jacob, grant me the spirit of perseverance in prayer, in the name of Jesus Christ;
    c. Lord Jesus, please give me the grace I need to live in complete surrender to Your most holy will;
    d. Lord Jesus, grant me the grace to remain faithful to You always.

14. Like a seed, I will always ..... *(pick from the following list),* no matter what the enemy throws at me—in the name of Jesus Christ.
    • Grow back to full life
    • Grow back stronger and bigger than before
    • Emerge with strength & hope
    • Have an unsurrendering purpose in life
    • Be glorious
    • Burst forth with life
    • Be more beautiful than before
    • Trust in God
    • Emerge a winner
    • Be alive

15. I plant snares and traps on every evil assignment against my life—I pray in the name of Jesus Christ.

16. I set fire on the enemy's strategies against me—I pray in the name of Jesus Christ.

17. May the warhorses of heaven tread down those who rise up to suppress my destiny, in the name of Jesus Christ.

18. Lord Jesus, grant that the Church of today develops the unsurrendering faith of the first century Church—I pray in the name of Jesus Christ.

19. Thank You, Lord Jesus Christ, for answering my prayers by coming to fight this battle and giving me victory.
    a. I am more than a conqueror in Christ (**Romans 8:37**)— in the name of Jesus Christ;
    b. Sing songs of victory to the Lord;
    c. Offer thanksgiving prayers with **Psalm 34** and **Psalm 107.**

20. I cover this prayer with the Most Precious Blood of Jesus Christ (7 times).

Chapter 5

TAKE AUTHORITY
AND CRUSH THEM

· · ◆ ◆ ◆ ◆ ◆ · ·

*"Then I saw an angel coming down from heaven,
holding in his hand the key to the bottomless pit and
a great chain. He seized the dragon, that ancient
serpent, who is the Devil and Satan, and bound him
for a thousand years, and threw him into the pit,
and locked and sealed it over him, so that he would
deceive the nations no more, until the thousand
years were ended."*

(Revelation 20:1-3)

(Other suggested Bible passages to read:
Genesis 3:15, Psalm 20:1-9, Romans 6:15-20, 2 Kings 11:1-4,
Ephesians 6:13-17, 2 Chronicles 20:1-29, 1 Samuel 17:1-58,
Psalm 68:1-35, Hebrews 11: 6-16, Joshua 10:1-42,
1 Kings 18:1-45).

DAY 10

Part 1: Reflection

I want to tell you something. It is regarding a truth I discovered
about life. The truth is that whatever you don't deal with in
your life will deal with you someday. This sounds hard but
its trueness is validated by the events of life. If you don't take
authority and deal with the devil, the devil will surely deal with

you in one way or another. If you address him today, he will not undress you tomorrow! Do not think that tyrants eat beans and rice; no, they eat lives and destinies of people. Their menu is flesh and blood! And a greater menace is that as soon as they get the opportunity to eat any destiny, they begin to position themselves in a way to access the victim's bloodline and then, like a locust, begin to eat away the "foliage" of their family tree. You don't give to such an enemy the opportunity to use you for dinner! He will want to consume all your blessings. Every Christian needs to understand that during their lifetime, the enemy will come to attack—maybe sickness, financial crisis, or family problems like divorce, betrayals or getting children hooked on drugs—but we have the responsibility to fight the enemy with the authority of Christ that has been given to us. It is important to understand that no matter the attacks of the enemy, we shall not fail to have deep faith in God—a faith that resists the enemy as we take an authority to crush him. In fact, spiritual warfare involves a confrontation with, taking authority over, and wrecking the kingdom of darkness in a way that causes them casualties. We must resist them with our prayers and faith in God (James 4:7). Our spiritual muscles become stronger over time as we continue to resist every move of the enemy.

Always remember that the devil has no authority over a true child of God— therefore, we should not allow him to trespass into the realms where his authority has been dismissed. Those who are not in Christ are slaves of the devil (Romans 6:15-20). Like Pharaoh, the enemy ruthlessly continues to demand that his slaves keep building his "pyramids" for him. He controls them. Don't allow the tyrants to have authority over you; instead, take authority over their dominion and enterprise.

Man's primary enemy is Satan. He oppresses people with sickness, disease, poverty and death. He is the reason why people are oppressed and feel caged-in by life situations. However, God has sent His anointed Son, Jesus Christ, who goes *"about doing good and healing all who were oppressed by the devil"* (Acts 10:38). He has all the authority and power to crush the devil—and He has given us that authority to overcome and crush the enemy in His name. Jesus, by His death on the Cross, crushed him [the devil] who holds the power of death **(Hebrews 2:14).** As the Scripture testifies, Jesus has come to destroy the devil and all his works **(1 John 3:8).** He comes to deliver us from the grip of the enemy. He is on a rescue mission to deliver us—He is our Mighty Warrior and Deliverer! Without Him, we are easy prey for the spiritual tyrants.

Our Lord, Jesus Christ, has openly stripped the devil of his powers and authority **(Colossians 2:15).** Taking the authority that Jesus Christ has given to us, we can decide that the head of the oppressor shall be crushed today. **Romans 16:20** says that *"The God of peace will shortly crush Satan under your feet."*

We must fight the oppressor. God has given us the mandate to subdue the earth and take authority over it, including *"the god of this world"* **(2 Corinthians 4:4).** So, we have to take authority over the tyrants. Jesus has also given us authority *"over all the power of the enemy"* **(Luke 10:19).** Even at the beginning of Christ's ministry, people were amazed as they witnessed Jesus, *"with authority... command[ing] even the unclean spirits"* and the evil spirits obeying the commands of Jesus Christ **(Mark 1:27).**

Sometimes, we forget that a major dimension of Christ's ministry was His battle with Satan. Immediately after His baptism, the Spirit led Jesus into the desert to confront Satan: we see Him casting out demons, healing the sick, and finally, through His Cross and resurrection, we see Him trample down the ancient foe once and for all. Like Jesus, we ought to offensively fight the tyrant's kingdom. Unfortunately, it seems that most of us only fight defensively—fighting back with wounds only after we have been given a stunning blow by the enemy. We have to take authority over the tyrants and crush them!

You can only have authority over what you have overcome. Therefore, we must, with prayer, take authority over the tyrants that Jesus has already overcome for us before we can protect our destinies. We are called to be militants — not in physical violence but in spiritual warfare **(Ephesians 6:12)**. We should, with the authority of Christ, shoot Satan out of the sky with our prayer missiles **(Luke 10:18)**. We should proceed to crush him under our feet with our God-given threshing-sledge legs **(Romans 16:20, Isaiah 41:15)**.

Now, listen: What is called "legs' in human anatomy is what God looked at and called your "threshing sledge"—and with it, *"you shall thresh the mountains and crush them, and you shall make the hills like chaff"* (Isaiah 41:15). So what are you waiting for before you begin to use your threshing sledge to level the mountains *"to the ground, and leave [them] in ashes"* (Jeremiah 51:25, GNT). We are to take authority and turn every demonic *"world upside down"* (Acts 17:6). As the children of Israel crossed the river Jordan in order to possess their promised land, so we are to possess our promised land by way of taking authority over the enemy in spiritual warfare.

The tyrants' only ambition is to steal, kill and to destroy **(John 10:10)**. They are all out to fight God's people. Like a flood, they release troubles upon the children of God in an effort to defeat them. But as God's battle-ax, we ought to rise to our feet and give a deathblow to Satan right on his head, and without mercy crush his head **(Genesis 3:15)**. Crushing the head of the oppressor is a command of God to us—not a suggestion! We should stand, and not waver in faith.

One of Bible's terrible women possessed by spiritual tyrants to oppress God's people was a woman called, *Athaliah*. The Scripture tells us in **2 Kings 11:1** that *"When Athaliah, Ahaziah's mother, saw that her son was dead, she set about to destroy all the royal family."* She was so brutal that she carried out a mission to massacre the rest of the royal family so she could take over the kingdom of Judah. However, seven years later, she was dethroned and killed. Her government was crushed into inexistence. God used four people (or groups of people) to bring this victory of justice:

1. Jehosheba risked her life to rescue a baby, her nephew, Joash, the rightful king **(2 Kings 11:2)**.

2. Others risked their lives daily for seven years by secretly caring for Joash **(2 Kings 11:3-4)**.

3. Jehoiada, the priest, risked his life by leading a coup d'état **(2 Kings11:4)**.

4. The captains of the temple guard risked their lives by swearing to support Jehoiada in the coup **(2 Kings 11:4)**.

The evil reign of Athaliah was defeated and crushed as God's warriors took authority. To crush the spiritual tyrants (or the Athaliahs in our time), we must have a blend of stubborn faith in God, irrepressible courage to fight the enemy, and unrelenting determination to persevere in the spiritual battle until the enemy is crushed. O yes, that's what we need. We shall proceed to take authority and crush them.

As we know, *"from the days of John the Baptist until now the kingdom of heaven has suffered violence, and the violent takes it by force"* (Matthew 11:12). It takes sure-fire prayers that reach the enemy's camp with crushing impacts to fully keep your blessings.

LET US PRAY!

1. Reflect on how this reflection on "Take Authority and Crush them" ministers to you.

2. Pray the Saint Michael the Archangel prayer (see page 17).

3. Pray the Anima Christi prayer (see page 18).

4. Pray **Psalm 3** (a prayer to strike the enemies).

5. As God's battle ax and weapons of war, I break down, crush, destroy, dam, and blow up all walls of protection around all witches, warlocks, wizards, Satanists, sorcerers, psychics and other messengers of the devil—in the name of Jesus Christ.

6. Begin to crush the enemy with every aggressiveness you can summon. In the name of Jesus Christ:
   a. I crush into pieces the gates of brass, and cut the bars of iron asunder **(Isaiah 45:2)**;
   b. I crush the enemies with the rod of iron and dash them into pieces like a potter's vessel **(Psalm 2:9)**;
   c. I crush the arm of the wicked **(Psalm 10:15)**;
   d. *"O God, break the teeth in their mouths"* (Psalm 58:6a);
   e. I crush and *"break out the great teeth of the young lions"* **(Psalm 58:6b)**;
   f. The oppressor is crushed to pieces **(Psalm 72:4)**;
   g. The arms, horns, foundations, and bows of the wicked are crushed **(Psalm 37:17)**;
   h. I crush into pieces the horse and the rider **(Jeremiah 51:21)** of all the militant evil kingdoms that are fighting me;
   i. I crush into pieces the captains and the rulers **(Jeremiah 51:23)** of every demonic entity that is standing between me and my promised land;
   j. The spoken Word of God out from my mouth is like a hammer that breaks into pieces the rocks of the evil kingdoms that are fighting me **(Jeremiah 23:29)**;
   k. With my feet, I *"shall thresh the mountains and crush them"* (Isaiah 41:15a);
   l. With my feet, I *"shall make the hills like chaff"* (Isaiah 41:15b) and will journey without any stumbling towards my promised land;

m. Every wall that is erected by the enemy against my life is crushed now **(Ezekiel 13:14)**;

n. Every altar that is erected by the enemy against my life is crushed **(Hosea 10:2)**;

o. Every idol or satanic image that is used against me is crushed **(Deuteronomy 7:5)**;

p. I crush the strength of leviathan's neck **(Psalm 18:40)**;

q. I crush the bones of every stubborn and unmovable leviathan **(Job 41:23)**;

r. I crush the teeth of the leviathans and pluck the spoil out of their mouths **(Job 41:15)**;

s. I crush the crown of pride in my life **(Isaiah 28:1)**.

7. Thank the Lord and cover this prayer with the Most Precious Blood of Jesus Christ (7 times).

DAY 11
Part 2: Warfare Prayers

Note:

- Be desperate to give the enemy a crushing deathblow. Don't relent!

- Offer God Spirit-filled praise and worship songs as the Spirit leads.

1. Confess and renounce each one of your sins before the Lord.
   a. Lord Jesus Christ, I now boldly approach Your throne of grace and mercy **(Hebrew 4:16)**;
   b. Pray **Psalm 51**;
   c. I am now willing to fully follow You all the rest of my life. I will now be guided by Your Holy Spirit from this moment on – and with the help of your grace, I will not cross back into the sin-filled life that I used to live in.

2. Pray the prayer of Saint Michael the Archangel (see page 17).

3. Pray the Anima Christi prayer (see page 18).

4. Begin to proclaim the Precious Blood of Jesus Christ as a weapon against the enemy.
    a. I cover myself and my household, and the environment of this prayer with the Most Precious Blood of Jesus Christ (7 times);
    b. I now plead the Blood of Jesus Christ over every inch of my spirit, my soul, my body, and every part of this entire house;

5. In the name of Jesus Christ, I decree that through this prayer:
    a. Every satanic chain on me must be broken;
    b. Every witchcraft hindrance must be lifted;
    c. Every demonic operation must come to a halt!

6. In the name of Jesus Christ, I decree to be annulled and crushed (pray very aggressively):
    a. Every power of the devil over the land of the city, state, and nation from border to border: East to West and North to South;
    b. Every curse and spell over my life, family, loved ones and this land;
    c. Every evil fruit that is around me and my family and loved ones.

7. Ask for Giant Warrior Angels to come down to assist you in this prayer. I make an alliance with the Heavenly Armies as I begin to pray:
    a. I put on the armor of God: the helmet of salvation, the breastplate of righteousness, the belt of truth, the sandals of the gospel of peace, the sword of the Spirit, and the shield of faith **(Ephesians 6:13-17).**

b. I am strong in the Lord and in the power of His might **(Ephesians 6:10)**;

c. Angels of the Living God, move your bulldozers into all the establishments of the devil and crush their territories;

d. O Angels of the Living God, smite them with flaming swords and hot thunderbolts of fire;

e. Let the Angels of God, with their two-edged swords, execute judgments against satanic forces.

8. I break and crush every demonic confederacy against my life, family, ministry, and Church, in the name of Jesus Christ.

9. Jesus, The Lion of the Tribe of Judah, roars through me against my enemies. Therefore, I am a threat to the kingdom of darkness— in the name of Jesus Christ.

10. In this prayer, ----- (*pick from the following list*), in the name of Jesus Christ.

a. I am releasing my prayer missiles to shoot down satanic messengers;

b. I shall crush the devil under my feet with my God-given threshing-sledge legs;

c. I shall level the mountains *"to the ground, and leave [them] in ashes"* **(Jeremiah 51:25, GNT)**;

d. I must possess my promised land through this spiritual warfare prayer;

e. I have the grace to crush demonic territories that I engage;

f. I close all satanic accesses and ports of entry into my life;

g. I close all entrance gates through which the devil wants to infiltrate and interfere with this prayer;

h. I cancel every charge and legal ground that the devil holds against me;

i. I take the enemies as prisoners of war;

    j.   The gates of hell will not prevail against this prayer;

    k.   The Lord Jesus Christ releases His sharp sword of fire out of His mouth against the enemy **(Revelation 19:15)**;

    l.   The enemies shall fall into the pits and nets they have set for me **(Psalm 35:7-8)**;

    m. I must prevail until I have victory.

11. The evil reign of Athaliah was defeated and crushed as God's warriors took authority. Begin to pray as follows:

    a.   Every spirit of Athaliah on a mission to massacre my destiny and close my lineage must not survive the heat of this prayer—in the name of Jesus Christ;

    b.   I take on an unrelenting determination to persevere in this battle until every "Athaliah" is crushed—in the name of Jesus Christ.

12. According to **Isaiah 7:2,** I decree that the heart of the tyrants shall shake *"as the trees of the forest shake before the wind."*

13. I trample upon and crush the head of every problem that I am going through, in the name of Jesus Christ.

14. In the name of Jesus Christ, I crush every satanic protocol that is affecting my breakthroughs.

15. *"When the king heard what the man of God cried out against the altar at Bethel, Jeroboam stretched out his hand from the altar, saying, "Seize him!" But the hand that he stretched out against him withered so that he could not draw it back to himself. The altar also was torn down, and the ashes poured out from the altar, according to the sign that the man of God had given by the word of the Lord"* **(1 Kings 13:4-5)**. Therefore, in the name of Jesus Christ, I decree that:

    a.   Every evil hand that is pointing at me must wither now;

    b.   Every altar that is raised against me must be torn down and crushed into pieces;

    c. I command the spirits behind the evil altars that are raised against me to be under house arrest now;

    d. I command every serpentine altar that is raised against me to catch fire and burn into ashes;

    e. As the wax is melted by fire, let all evil altars speaking against my destiny melt by fire;

    f. I command all satanic altars that are raised against me to stop functioning from today till the second coming of my Lord Jesus Christ.

16. I command all....(*pick from the following list*) assigned for use against me to be crushed into pieces by Jesus bulldozer— in the name of Jesus Christ.
    - Weapons and ammunitions
    - Witchcraft vehicles and armored tanks
    - Witchcraft covens and dominions
    - Satanic computers and databases
    - Occult temples and strongholds
    - Monitoring gadgets and systems

17. I take authority and begin to crush every ....(*pick from the following list*) embargo that is placed on my life, in the name of Jesus Christ.
    - Witchcraft
    - Generational & ancestral
    - Evil load

18. In the name of Jesus Christ, I crush defeat with victory over the tyrants.

19. In the name of Jesus Christ, I crush the head of every serpent in my father's house.

20. Thank You, Lord Jesus Christ, for giving me the grace to take authority and crush all the invisible enemies that are fighting against me.

    a. Sing songs of victory to the Lord;

    b. Offer thanksgiving prayers with Psalm 149 and **Psalm 150.**

21. I cover this prayer with the Most Precious Blood of Jesus Christ (7 times).

Chapter 6

SUMMON THAT TYRANT!

· • ◆ ◆ ◆ ◆ • ·

"When the king heard what the man of God cried out against the altar at Bethel, Jeroboam stretched out his hand from the altar, saying, "Seize him!" But the hand that he stretched out against him withered so that he could not draw it back to himself. The altar also was torn down, and the ashes poured out from the altar, according to the sign that the man of God had given by the word of the Lord."

(1 Kings 13:4-5)

(Other suggested Bible passages to read:
2 Samuel 5: 17-21, 2 Samuel 24:25, 1 Kings 18:16-40).

DAY 12

Part 1: Reflection

One of the common practices in the kingdom of darkness is to raise an altar of darkness against the children of God so as to afflict them. In this chapter's lead Scripture **(1 Kings 13:4-5)**, we see that King Jeroboam stretched out his hand from his evil altar against a man of God, saying, *"Seize him!"* **(1 Kings 13:4)**. From his altar, he wanted to spiritually arrest or seize the man of God. This is a fight of powers behind altars: altars of gods against Altar of God—and of course, God wins because the power behind God's Altar is the all-surpassing power of God. The plan of King Jeroboam against the man of God backfired against him as *"The hand that he stretched out against him [the man of God] withered so that he could not draw it back to himself"* (1 Kngs 13:4). The power of God goes further to destroy Jeroboam's evil altar: *"The altar also was torn down, and the ashes poured out from the altar, according to the sign that the man of God had given by the word of the Lord"* (1 Kings 13:5). That's how powerful the power of God is; but, how many Christians believe that this power is at work in them? Would I assume that you have an Altar of God in your house? I hope your response is yes!

Like King Jeroboam, the Philistines came to the battlefield to fight the Israelites with their idols, charms, and altars **(2 Samuel 5: 21)**. It was one of the means which the wicked uses against the righteous. Those in the kingdom of darkness can not only monitor people from their altars or summon the spirit of people to their altars, but can also project evil forces to go out and harm people. Many destinies have been nailed down to stagnation by way of summoning them to demonic altars. I once listened to the narration of a man's confession whose evil altar was an airport from where he flies out to attend night meetings of witches and from where he also flies to attack people.

There is power behind every altar! King Jeroboam, an unbeliever, knew that! Many Christians are yet to realize this truth. If we know the power of God's Altar, then we shall boldly confront and frazzle every demonic engagement. There is great power in the Altar of God. Your Altar of prayer can intercept demonic projections.

My dear, evil altars are real! I once had a vision in which I saw a lady standing helplessly before a spiritual judge presiding over a spiritual court session taking place at an altar of judgment against her. I heard the counts against her and before she could open her mouth to say a word in defense, the spiritual judge declared a sentence against her saying, *"You have been sentenced to remain single forever."* She was crying bitterly. Poor lady! That spiritual judge is a spiritual tyrant mortgaging an evil decree against her marriage. This lady (who was single and a little advanced in age) was summoned to a demonic judicial system for judgment and condemnation. She was sentenced to remain single for the rest of her life. What a wickedness! We may need to be reminded that the Jewish elders brought Jesus to Pilate's court, and asked Pontius Pilate to judge and condemn Jesus, accusing Him of claiming to be the King of the Jews. This is the way of the spiritual tyrants: to summon the children of God to a place of spiritual judgment and condemnation. Even Pilate summoned Jesus to the Praetorium **(John 18:33)**. Is there a possibility that what you are going through now is as a result of being spiritually summoned to the court of the spiritual tyrants?

When the enemy summons a child of God to their altar, the aim is clear: judgment, condemnation, and affliction. It must be known that altars are the devil's asset against the Church. Coincidentally, the Altar of Calvary is also a spiritual asset of the Church against the kingdom of darkness. Spiritual tyrants cannot stand the Altar of our God. Prayer warriors are yet to fully realize that summoning the devil and his cohorts to the foot of the Cross of Jesus Christ is a powerful weapon of prayer against demonic forces. Hence, we should take advantage of this great weapon of warfare to disadvantage the hordes of spiritual tyrants against us! In this chapter, we shall be bold to summon every spiritual tyrant to the Altar of Calvary for judgment, condemnation, and total destruction (every Altar of God is one with the Altar of Calvary).

The effectiveness of this warfare strategy is based on the fact that upon His sacrificial death on the Cross, Jesus Christ destroyed all the works of the devil, crushing his head and disarming him of his deadly power. It was on the Cross that Jesus Christ took away each and every judgment, condemnation, and punishment passed on us by the devil. Therefore, while at the foot of the Cross and facing the Cross' four cardinal directions, we shall summon the tyrants from the North, South, East, and the West to perish at the foot of the Cross! In the authority of Christ, we shall summon to the Altar of God for judgment, every messenger of Satan or deity empowering satanic altars, shrines, temples and dominions.

At the risk of repeating myself, let me repeat myself: We must attack the spiritual tyrants by boldly summoning them to the foot of the Cross (the Altar of Calvary) for judgment and de-struction! We shall call upon the Holy Spirit to blow away to the abyss or to the foot of the Cross, every evil force projected to harm us. Following the war tactics of Prophet Elisha, it is a welcome warfare strategy to summon the tyrants to the Altar of God and strike them with blindness **(2 Kings 6:18)**. Every prayer meant to disgrace the tyrants must be done aggressively—and so you must fight against them like a tyrant too!

LET US PRAY!

1. Reflect on how this reflection on "Summon that Tyrant" ministers to you.

2. Pray the Saint Michael the Archangel prayer (see page 17).

3. Pray the Anima Christi prayer (see page 18).

4. Pray **Psalm 109** (a prayer against the enemies).

5. Close your eyes. Conceive yourself at the sacrificial Altar of Jesus Christ at Calvary. Now begin to pray in the name of Jesus Christ:

a. I stand in the presence of our Lord Jesus Christ, at the foot of the Cross, and I submit to the authority of His Majesty as I make this prayer;

b. Ask God to lead you in this spiritual battlefield that you are getting into now, and to arm you with the sword of the Holy Spirit, which is The Word of God. Begin to sing songs that connote the Blood of Jesus Christ (e.g. "*There is Power mighty in the Blood*");

c. Lord, I humbly prostrate myself at the foot of the Cross of Jesus Christ, the Son of God, who came in the flesh (then begin to pray as follows):

    i. I cover myself with the Blood and water that are gushing forth from the side of Jesus Christ *(repeat 3 times)*;

    ii. O Lord Jesus Christ, may Your all-surpassing power powering Your Altar destroy all evil altars that are erected within a 200-mile radius from this location of prayer.

d. Blood of Jesus Christ, protect me from all the attacks of all spiritual tyrant forces and from all their influences!

    i. By the power of the Blood of Jesus Christ, I close every pathways that have allowed Satan and his co-tyrants to get into my life;

    ii. By the power of the Most Precious Blood of Jesus Christ, I annul every legal right that the tyrants have over my life;

    iii. I expose myself to God's divine radiations emanating from the Sacred Heart of Jesus Christ;

    iv. May the gushing Blood of Jesus Christ cover my family, my friends, my relationships, my house, my properties and all that belong to me;

    v. Let the Blood of Jesus Christ bring upon me the manifestations of the victory of Christ on the Cross of Calvary;

    vi. Let the rays of healing from Christ's pierced hands envelop me and my family;

e. I tap into the Blood flowing from Christ's head, hands, feet, back, and side. Pray the following prayers (making each prayer in the name of Jesus Christ):

    i. The Blood from Christ's head when the thorns pierced His Sacred head shields my head from every fiery arrow of the evil one **(Ephesians 6:16)**;

    ii. The Blood from Christ's pierced hands frees me from the chains on my hands **(Jeremiah 40:4)**;

    iii. The Blood from Christ's pierced feet will *"break the chains that hold us back and throw off the ropes that tie us down"* **(Psalm 2:3, NCV)**;

    iv. The Blood from Christ's lacerated Body heals me and destroys every sting of death;

    v. The Blood from Christ's pierced side covers me and my family, and we cannot be summoned by the kingdom of darkness;

f. In the name of Jesus Christ (as I take a stand at the foot of the Cross), I command every demonic element to go immediately under the foot of the Cross of Jesus Christ to be disposed of according to God's Holy Will. Then begin to pray as follows, ending every prayer with *"in the Name of Jesus Christ"*;

    i. I bind all evil spirits (spirits of the tyrants) hiding in the air, water, earth, under the earth and infernal world. I invoke the Precious Blood of Jesus Christ gushing forth from the Body of Jesus in the air, the atmosphere, the water, the land and its fruits. I command you all to perish;

    ii. I bind all demonic spies sent against me from the headquarters of spiritual tyrants. I command you all to perish;

    iii. In the name of Jesus Christ, I break, I shatter, and I cancel every curse, betrayal, enchantment, spell, trap, lie, obstacle, evil arrows, hereditary blockage (known or unknown), manipulations or evil desire projected at me by spiritual tyrants to cause me misfortune or any disorder;

    iv. In the name of Jesus Christ, I cancel every attachment to spiritual tyrants and I disengage myself today from any known or unknown association or relationship with the powers of evil.

  g. Jesus Christ has disarmed the devil of his deadly power. Therefore, Satan has no power over my life.

6.   Thank the Lord and cover this prayer with the Most Precious Blood of Jesus Christ (7 times).

DAY 13

Part 2: Warfare Prayers

Note:

- A well-defined strategy is needed to win the spiritual forces confronting us. One of such strategies is to summon the spiritual enemies to the Altar of the Living God to be disposed of according to His will.

- It is recommended that this prayer be made before an Altar of God.

1.   *"Great is the Lord, and greatly to be praised; His greatness is unsearchable"* **(Psalm 145:3).** Let this opening Psalm lead you spontaneously into praising and worshipping God as the Holy Spirit leads you (avoid distractions).

2.   Pray for God's mercy.
    a. O Lord, I lay down at Your feet and ask for the forgiveness of my sins;

    b. O Lord Jesus, may Your ocean of mercy wash away my sins;

    c. "Eternal Father, I offer you the Body and Blood, Soul and Divinity of Your Dearly Beloved Son, Our Lord, Jesus Christ, in atonement for our sins and those of the whole world. For the sake of His sorrowful Passion, have mercy on us and on the whole world"—St. Maria Faustina Kowalska of the Blessed Sacrament;

    d. "Eternal God, in whom mercy is endless and the treasury of compassion inexhaustible, look kindly upon us and increase Your mercy in us, that in difficult moments we might not despair nor become despondent, but with great confidence submit ourselves to Your holy will, which is Love and Mercy itself"—St. Maria Faustina Kowalska of the Blessed Sacrament;

    e. Pray **Psalm 51** for the forgiveness of sins.

3. Pray the prayer of Saint Michael the Archangel (see page 17).

4. Pray the Anima Christi prayer (see page 18).

5. Pray and ask the power of the Holy Spirit to rest upon you as you pray this prayer (pray as the Spirit leads you).

6. The Word of God says in **2 Samuel 24:25** that, *"David built there an altar to the Lord, and offered burnt offerings and offerings of well-being. So the Lord answered his supplication for the land, and the plague was averted from Israel."* Therefore, in the name of Jesus Christ:

    a. O God, as You *"answered his supplication for the land,"* so may You answer my prayers;

    b. I command every plague and destruction targeting my life and family to be averted from us;

    c. O Lord Jesus, may this sacrifice of prayers at this Altar be *"offerings of well-being"* for me and my family;

    d. I cancel every evil sacrifice empowering evil altars against my life and family;

    e. You evil altars, there shall be no sacrifices on you again!

    f. You satanic altars, there shall be no worship at you again!

7. Today I put under the Sovereignty of our Lord Jesus Christ everything that belongs to me (both material and spiritual) and which was subject to the jurisdiction of satan and his co-tyrants—in the name of Jesus Christ.

8. Lord Jesus Christ, You know the troubles that these tyrants have brought to my life all these years. Now, I lay these burdens at the foot of the Cross (present the situations to the Lord and leave them at the foot of the Cross). They are no more mine—in the name of Jesus Christ.

9. I beseech You, Lord Jesus Christ, let the open deep wounds on Your Body caused by being scourged with whips heal all the wounds in my life that the tyrants have caused me—in the name of Jesus Christ.

    a. Heal the pains in my wounded and bleeding heart caused by the wears and tears of the tyrant spirits against my life all these years;

    b. I, therefore, offer You the condition of my heart: Accept it and give me the sentiments of Your Divine Heart, which can neither be corrupted nor destroyed by the enemies.

10. In the name of Jesus Christ, I command all wandering messengers of the satanic kingdom that want to alter the effectiveness of this prayer to be paralyzed and be frozen to stillness.

11. Begin to pray against all the communication devices used by the messengers of Satan, proclaiming "in the name of Jesus Christ" after each prayer point.

a. I command every communication between the messengers of Satan and their evil altars to seize;

b. I command every communication among the messengers of Satan to seize, and never to provide any mutual aid to each other anymore;

c. I command every communication between evil altars of satanic messengers to seize and never to communicate with each other again;

d. I decree that the messengers of Satan have no legal right to communicate with me anymore;

e. I plant the Cross of Jesus Christ inside me and inside all my past and future generations:

   i. And by so doing, I cease all direct communication of evil transfers between these generations;

   ii. And I decree that all these communications are now filtered through the most precious Blood of our Lord Jesus Christ.

12. In the name of Jesus Christ, I command every wandering messenger of Satanic forces targeting my life and my blessings to begin to melt right now like wax before the fire **(Psalm 68:2).**

13. In the name of Jesus Christ, I command every poisoned arrow of the spiritual tyrants (and other messengers of Satan) targeting me and my family to backfire (repeat 3 times).

14. Satanic sacrifices at crossroads are often used to summon demons from the North, South, East, and West against a person—so pray against such satanic summon from the four cardinal points of the earth. Therefore, in the name of Jesus Christ, I decree that:

a. The Altar of Jesus Christ's sacrifice on the hill of Calvary has made powerless and useless every evil altar raised at Crossroads to summon me by satanic sacrifices;

    b. Every spiritual tyrant summoning my spirit to any Crossroad is reversed forever.

15. In the name of Jesus Christ, I decree that every:
    a. Spiritual tyrant be chased from my heart, my house, and members of my household to the abyss and be chained there forever;
    b. Spiritual domain of the spiritual tyrants in the celestial spaces, sacred rivers, sacred mountains, and the evil forests be burned into ashes by the consuming fire of the Holy Spirit.

16. *"As the enemy came down toward him, Elisha prayed to the LORD, 'Strike this army with blindness'"* **(2 Kings 6:18).** Therefore, in the name of Jesus Christ, I command every spiritual tyrant summoning my spirit to their evil altar to go blind.

17. By the power of the Most High God who defeated you Satan and triumphed over you on the gibbet of the Cross on Calvary, I summon you tyrant spirits to fly from the North, South, East, and West to the foot of the Cross of Jesus Christ for eternal damnation— in the name of Jesus Christ. Now, begin to pray aggressively (using the name of Jesus Christ):
    a. Be bound eternally;
    b. Be disgraced and be destroyed and never to rise again;
    c. Be rendered impotent;
    d. Begin to vomit all my blessings that you have swallowed;
    e. Begin to release my blessings that you have entrapped for ages;
    f. Let the hammer of the Almighty God smash your heads;
    g. Let the thunder of God smite you all into irreparable pieces;
    h. Dry up, wither, and burn to ashes!
    i. Let the Blood of Jesus Christ gushing forth from the Cross

destroy every tyrant spirit. Begin to declare aggressively (make each prayer in the name of Jesus Christ):

    i.   I possess my possessions stolen by the spiritual tyrants;

    ii.   I withdraw my glory and breakthroughs from every evil altar;

    iii.   I withdraw all my blessings withheld by the tyrants.

18. Begin to summon every asset of the tyrants to the Altar of Calvary for destruction (make each prayer in the name of Jesus Christ):

    a.   I summon to the Altar of Calvary and set on fire every stronghold, shrine, temple, evil altar, witchcraft coven, charms, demonic priest, and deity used by the tyrants against me;

    b.   I destroy every satanic power representing me from every evil altar;

    c.   I destroy every evil altar speaking death over my life.

19. Summon to the Altar and pray for the repentance of the human servants of Satan (present their names if you know them) who are occultists, wizards and witches, members of satanic sects and esoteric orders, voodoo and juju practitioners, and such likes. Also pray that if they refuse to repent, persisting in doing evil to you or other children of God, let their own curses which they projected towards others begin to turn against them— *"For all who take the sword will perish by the sword"* (Matthew 26:52).

20. I refuse to be a toy in the hands of the spiritual tyrants!

    a.   I refuse to appear in a place of spiritual judgment and condemnation—in the name of Jesus Christ;

    b.   I decree that my spirit shall not ..... *(pick from the following list)* when summoned—in the name of Jesus Christ;

- Appear in demonic mirrors
- Appear in demonic altars
- Engage with a demonic spouse
- Drink the water of bitterness
- Be nailed down to stagnation
- Appear in satanic courts
- Eat the bread of sorrows
- Appear before any deity

21. Deliver me, O Lord, from all the spiritual tyrant forces trying to get into my dreams to cause me nightmares, in the name of Jesus Christ.

22. Lord Jesus Christ, I have faith in Your unfailing Power to bless me with the grace to walk out with the answers to my prayers, in the name of Jesus Christ.

23. Thank You, Lord Jesus Christ, for answering my prayers and giving me victory.
    a. Sing songs of victory to the Lord;
    b. Offer thanksgiving prayers with **Psalm 100** and **Psalm 136**

24. I cover this prayer with the Most Precious Blood of Jesus Christ (7 times).

Chapter 7
RETURN FIRE FOR FIRE

$\cdots \bullet \blacklozenge \bullet \cdots$

"And war broke out in heaven; Michael and his angels fought against the dragon. The dragon and his angels fought back, but they were defeated, and there was no longer any place for them in heaven. The great dragon was thrown down, that ancient serpent, who is called the devil and Satan, the deceiver of the whole world— he was thrown down to the earth, and his angels were thrown down with him...for the accuser of our comrades has been thrown down, who accuses them day and night before our God."

(Revelation 12:7-10)

(Other suggested Bible passages to read:
Jeremiah 30:16-17, Number 23:23, Psalm 7:15-16, I Kings13:1 – 4;
2 King 19:1 – 37, Job 7:9 – 11; Psalm 2, Psalm 11:6, Isaiah 29:6;
Psalm 33:10, Psalm 34:21; Psalm 35; Psalm 36:11-12, Psalm 59;
Psalm 58:1 – 11).

DAY 14
Part 1: Reflection

Read the above Scripture again **(Revelation 12:7-10)**. Do you notice that *"war broke out in heaven"*? **(Revelation 12:7)**. Yes, Lucifer broke rank with God and established his own army in opposition to God. This was the first war that took place since creation. It was also the first rebellion, the first revolution, and the first illegal and overt seizure of a state apparatus—an attempt to overthrow the Heavenly Government of our God. I believe this was an attempted coup d'état. This is the genesis of war and dissention in all creation. But I have a concern here: Why would Heaven, of all places, be a place to hear of war, rebellion or attempted coup d'état? How come war first broke out in Heaven—and not on earth or in the cosmos, or in any other place? This concern is heightened when one considers that Heaven is the eternal City and a dwelling place of the Almighty God.

We know Heaven as a peaceful place, and not a place of war or dissention! We look forward to Heaven as a reward for our faithfulness, notwithstanding the troubles we go through now. 1 **Peter 5:10** testifies of this as thus: *"And after you have suffered for a little while, the God of all grace, who has called you to His eternal glory in Christ, will Himself restore, support, strengthen, and establish you."* Indeed, Heaven is God's settlement for the just. Jesus Christ Himself comforts His suffering people in **John 14:2-3** with the promise that He goes to prepare a place in Heaven for them where *"He will wipe every tear from their eyes. Death will be no more; mourning and crying and pain will be no more, for the first things have passed away."* (**Revelation 21:4**). Undoubtedly, Heaven is a place where there is no sorrow. But I am concerned that war broke out in such a City of eternal peace— because a tyrant invented war there. Don't give the devil a place in your haven lest he invents crisis there.

War broke out because a tyrant emerged in heaven. The war is a war of who should be worshipped—God or Lucifer.[1] Lucifer, now Satan, exalts himself to become like God so that he would be worshiped, but we know that our God is the only One who is worthy to be worshiped. Although Satan was dethroned from

---

1. Angel Lucifer became Satan or the devil, the Chief Tyrant, when he took the path of rebellion against God.

heaven, yet, on earth, he seeks to be worshiped. In exalting himself, he attempts to dissuade people to worship him. All forms of satanic system of worship is meant to takeover God's authority over us and keep people ignorant of the truth of the Gospel. Satan knows that all people were created as vessels of worship and—whether they realize it or not—they will worship something. Be it known to us that every person on earth is either worshiping the true and living God, or worshiping Satan and his demonic forces—either overtly or covertly through sin (whether they be of omission or commission).

One of the characteristic nature of the spiritual tyrants is that they bring war where war does not exist—be it in a peaceful marriage, lovely family or prosperous venture. Like Jonah, a tyrant comes into a peaceful sailing ship and raises an altar of storm, and refuses to leave it until a wreck takes place. Are you familiar with a marriage wrecked with a divorce? A tyrant can ruin someone's health with sickness. A tyrant has nothing good to offer but sorrow and bitterness. A war erupted in Heaven because an Angel turned into a tyrant. Who is the "angel" in your life that has turned into a tyrant? I recall the agony of a sister who was crying because the "angel" she married has become a tyrant.

When the enemy invented war in Heaven, God made one decision: Return Fire for Fire! In this historic battle, God returned war with war. It was through war that Heaven dethroned the tyrant in their midst. Spiritual warfare demands a returned fire, not a retreat. It is by war—I mean spiritual warfare— that you will be able to keep your blessings. It was by way of warfare that Heaven obtained their victory over the angel-turned-tyrant in their territory. We have no option on earth than to return fire for fire! May I remind you that it was when the sailors got rid of Jonah in their ship that the storm rested.

You must confront the Jonah in your own ship, and throw him away before you can have your peace. That is war, not negotiation! In spiritual battles, we anchor on Christ's victory over the devil on the Cross in order to obtain the same victory of Archangel Michael and his co-Angels when they returned fire for fire in Heaven. God is the One who placed us in this time, so He gives us what we need to return fire for fire.

I wish to submit a thesis here that it is by war, and only by war, that you will be able to get rid of that spiritual tyrant in your life. It is by war that you will recover your stolen glory—not by appeasing the devil with sacrifices or by pleading with him to leave you alone. Like Jesus, we must engage the enemy in spiritual warfare or else we lose the war. Think of it: God needed peace in His Heaven—but did God plead or lobby with Satan to leave Heaven? Of course, no!

God is All Powerful and would have blown Satan out of Heaven with a puff from His nostrils, yet He ordered Michael and his legion of Angels to go for war. If you want peace, fight for it; fight the tyrant—don't run away from him! This principle has transcended through the ages with unfailing and effective results. We must, therefore, fight the devil outrightly.

One man patiently waited for his turn in a long line during one of my consultation sessions. When he came, I could see a troubled man in his face. I expected a long list of woes but he surprised me with only one request—*"Brother Uwakwe, please, plead with the devil to leave me alone and mind his own business! That's all I want!"* After laughing, I told him that I'd not plead with the devil to leave him alone, but enlighten him on the need to be a fighter, to return fire for fire. We don't plead with the devil. We take our God-given authority over him! We need to understand that the way out of our predicament is to summon the effrontery and boldly fight the spiritual tyrants before we can have our victory.

I want to tell you a hard truth, but not without you reading **Revelation 12:7-10** again. Do you observe that it was by a persevering spirit of tenacity that Michael and his Angels got rid of the tyrant in Heaven? The Scripture tells us that as Michael and his angels fought against the dragon, the dragon and his angels also fought back. However, with the superior weapons of Heaven, Michael and his warring Angels resisted the tyrants until *"they were defeated, and there was no longer any place for them in Heaven. The great dragon was thrown down."* **(Revelation 12:8-9)**. What a silent reminder to us that it is with an unrelenting audacity that we shall resist the tyrants to the point of submission. My friend, the hard truth I want to tell you is that you must be a fighter in order to keep your testimony.

David went out to fight Goliath before Israel got their victory. Gideon had to fight the Midianites before victory came to God's people. And so was Samson! What I mean is that you are going to fight a tyrant, and you must be determined to resist him until the fight is over. That's what I mean! The war is over only when you either kill or dethrone the tyrant. Tyrants don't yield easily; they are "diehard" spirits. It is the nature of the spiritual tyrants to fight. It is also by a fight that you can destroy them. They yield and flee only when they meet a man who resists their mission with prayer. Scripture admonishes us to resist him and then he will flee **(James 4:7)**.

You cannot escape the tyranny of the tyrant without a fight. You cannot plunder the tyrant's territory as to recover your stolen testimonies without a fight. My dear, you cannot walk in dominion while fearing to confront the tyrant! You must be willing to weary him with your prayer. A Persian tyrant trapped the Angel bringing Daniel's blessings but the testimony of Daniel 10:1-21 reveals that it was through the persevering prayer of Daniel that he was able to obtain his victory over the tyrant. It cannot be argued that prayer brings victory!

It cannot be overemphasized that this is not a game for the gentleman. Jacob did not play a gentleman when he wanted his blessings from the Angel of God **(Genesis 32:22-31)**. Although Jacob did not fight a devil in **Genesis 32** account before getting his mogul blessings, yet it was through a persevering fight with an Angel that he actually obtained the blessings that God promised even before his birth **(Genesis 25:23)**. Jacob laid hold of the promise of God through a night of wrestling-prayer.

The blessings of God are released into our lives through prayer. Every prayer of faith that we make brings us closer to our victory over the tyrant. Do you still remember the song: "What a friend we have in Jesus" by Joseph M. Scriven? It ends with: "What a privilege to carry everything to God in prayer!" Let us carry everything to God in prayer!

We must be people of spiritual warfare to stay on top. We have to face the enemy and engage him in warfare. Let the kingdom of darkness feel the crescendo of hammer blows from your prayer! It is with prayer that you can detonate the satanic timed bombs of calamity over your family. Don't underestimate the power of one prayer bullet to spoil the devil's agenda to kill, steal, and destroy you **(John 10:10)**! Goliath fired at David with words of curses in the name of his gods **(1 Samuel 17:43)**—but David fired back with a stone that got Goliath down. That is "return fire for fire!"

It cannot be argued that the contemporary Christians are not committed in prayer like the Christians of the Apostolic days. The result is that the enemy has brought big storms that carried many lives into many heaps of rubbles—misfortune, war, death, calamity, distress, sorrow, sadness, misery, grief, starvation, and wretchedness. However, if for every arrow the devil fires at us we fire back at him with God's weapons of warfare, we cannot be his victims. So, it is alright to "return fire for fire!" *"With unceasing blows"* (Isaiah 14:6), let our rockets of fire be released against the kingdom of darkness. In the end, prayer promises a winning song of victory!

Before we come to the end of this chapter, I invite you to ponder on these Biblical cases: Jeroboam released a deadly arrow from his evil altar to seize the man of God from Judah, but it backfired against him, crippling him (1 Kings 13:1-4) —a return of fire for fire! Haman plotted to kill all the Jews but Queen Esther prayed and fasted (a return of fire for fire), and the Jews were saved while Haman died in the gallows that he had prepared for Mordechai (Esther 7:10). King Sennacherib of Assyria unleashed serious threats on Jerusalem (2 Kings 18:17-37), but when King Hezekiah in 2 Kings 19:14 tabled the matter before the Lord *"the Lord sent an Angel, who annihilated all the fighting men and the commanders and officers in the camp of the Assyrian king... and when he [King Sennacherib] went into the temple of his god, some of his sons... cut him down with the sword"* (2 Chronicles 32: 21). The Lord destroyed the Assyrian armies and their King (Sennacherib of Assyria) because King Hezekiah in Isaiah 37:21 prayed to God concerning the situation...only then did God return fire for fire. In these cases—and other cases that time and space would not allow me to mention here—the Lord Himself took over, returning fire for fire! Is it not time to hear your own victory story? I believe that this is the time!

LET US PRAY!

1. Reflect on how this reflection on "Return Fire for Fire" ministers to you.

2. Pray the Saint Michael the Archangel prayer (see page 17).

3. Pray the Anima Christi prayer (see page 18).

4. Pray Psalm 83 (a prayer to frustrate wicked conspiracy).

5. To all demonic artillery fired against my life and my loved ones: BACKFIRE with fire, BACKFIRE with shame, and BACKFIRE with destruction, NOW, in the name of Jesus Christ.

6. You arrows of ..... (*pick from the following list*) fired at me, backfire in the name of Jesus Christ.

   - Errors and mistakes
   - Untimely death
   - Non-achievement
   - Repeated problems
   - Ridicule
   - Effigy
   - Confusion & discouragement
   - Enchantment & incantation
   - Poverty & tragedy
   - Torment & pain
   - Hatred & rejection
   - Strange wind
   - Judgment
   - Lamentation
   - Sickness
   - Evil marks
   - Evil shadow
   - The unknown

7. Command every arrow fired against you to backfire.
   a. I command every evil arrow that is fired at..... (*pick from the following list*) to go back to the sender(s), in the name of Jesus Christ, Amen.

      - My health
      - My occupation
      - My relationships
      - My rising up
      - My family
      - My plans
      - My destiny
      - My welfare
      - My work
      - My resources
      - My career
      - My advancement
      - My breakthrough
      - My opportunities

   b. I especially surrender -------(Continue to surrender every other area of your life that is attacked by the tyrants. Ask the Holy Spirit to bring them to your mind).

8. Pray very aggressively! Your declaration after each prophetic action listed below shall be (the RESPONSE): "Arrows from the kingdom of darkness, backfire in the name of Jesus Christ, Amen".

   a. Grab your head with your two hands and pray the RESPONSE;

   b. Lay your hands on your chest and pray the RESPONSE;

   c. Lay your hands upon your stomach and pray the RESPONSE;

   d. Lay your hands on your two legs and pray the RESPONSE;

   e. Lay your hands on any other part of your body you desire a release and pray the RESPONSE.

9. Thank the Lord and cover this prayer with the Most Precious Blood of Jesus Christ (7 times).

DAY 15
Part 2: Warfare Prayers

Note:

- In spiritual warfare, it is either you kill or you be killed. So, use this prayer to fight with every determination to stay alive.

- *"Prepare war, stir up the warriors. Let all the soldiers draw near, let them come up"* **(Joel 3:9).**

1. Offer Spirit-filled praise and worship songs to God as the Spirit leads. Suggested songs of war to get started with are:

   a. *"Let God arise and my enemies be scattered, let God, let Jesus arise"*

    b. *"O Lord, come down and manifest Your Power..."*
    c. *"Jesus is a mighty God (X2)...evil power bow before Him"*

2. Use **Psalm 51** to ask God for the forgiveness of your sins.

3. Pray the prayer of Saint Michael the Archangel (see page 17).

4. Pray the Anima Christi prayer (see page 18).

5. I cover myself and my household, our destinies and divine helpers, as well as the environment of this prayer with the Most Precious Blood of Jesus Christ (7 times).

6. Pray with **2 Chronicles 20:12:** *"Our God, will you not judge them? For we have no power to face this vast army that is attacking us. We do not know what to do, but our eyes are on you."* Make the following prayers "in the name of Jesus Christ":
    a. Rescue us, O Lord, from the hands of the tyrants for the sake of Your mighty name;
    b. You devil, hear me: *"Devise a plan, but it will be thwarted; state a proposal, but it will not stand, for God is with us"* **(Isaiah 8:10, NKJV);**
    c. You devil, hear me: Your plans against me shall come to nothing **(Psalms 33:10);**
    d. You devil, hear me: The craftiness of your hands to stop my testimonies are thwarted **(Job 5:12);**
    e. You devil, hear me: *"How the oppressor has ceased! How his insolence has ceased! The Lord has broken the staff of the wicked..."* **(Isaiah 14:6).**

7. Every power that is deciding my case at the evil altar, catch fire, in the name of Jesus Christ.

8. Loving Lord Jesus, You destroyed the power of death on the Cross. You triumphed over the powers of darkness. Make

the following prayers "in the name of Jesus Christ":

a. I call upon Your powerful name for my deliverance;

b. I submit to Your authority and resist the devil in Your name;

c. I believe that You have delivered me from the domain of darkness and transferred me to Your Kingdom of Light (Colossians 1:13). I give You all the glory, Lord!

9. In the misery of Israel and Judah, God promised restoration through Prophet Jeremiah as thus: *"Therefore all who devour you shall be devoured, and all your foes, every one of them, shall go into captivity; those who plunder you shall be plundered, and all who prey on you I will make a prey. For I will restore health to you, and your wounds I will heal, says the Lord, because they have called you an outcast: "It is Zion; no one cares for her!"* (Jeremiah 30:16-17). Make each prayer in the name of Jesus Christ, saying:

a. O Lord Jesus, deploy Your Holy Angels to plunder and devour every spiritual tyrant that is on assignment to plunder and devour my life, family and the works of my hands;

b. O Lord Jesus, lead every one of these tyrants that is pursuing my destiny into their own captivity;

c. O Lord Jesus, prey on all tyrants that are preying on me and on the resources that You have given to me;

d. O Lord Jesus, restore all that the tyrants stole from me, including my health:

   i. Lord, You have heard it from the mouth of the tyrant concerning me, saying: *"No one cares for her!"* (Jeremiah 30:17). Lord, prove them wrong by healing me, please;

   ii. I take hold of Your Word in John 11:4 to decree that *"This illness does not lead to death; rather it is for God's glory, so that the Son of God may be glorified through it."*

e. Heal every deep wound caused by the tyrants in my life that are still holding me to the past:

    i. Lord, I surrender my entire life to You, the past, the present and the future— I surrender all to You today with all my heart;

    ii. Lord Jesus, please come into my heart in a deeper way to heal every open wound and bandage my bleeding heart;

    iii. I invite You into every secret places of my heart that is darkened by unforgiveness;

    iv. With Your Light, break down every veil of resentment and emotional hurt that I am still carrying in my heart. I hold nothing back.

10. O God, You are my strength and consolation. Keep me steadfast in faith in the midst of all the trials of life so that I may always be faithful and pleasing to You—in the name of Jesus Christ.

11. O Lord Jesus, grant me the grace to successfully navigate through every rough terrain and then experience the thrill of conquering all the challenges that the spiritual tyrants bring my way—in the name of Jesus Christ.

12. Lord Jesus, You know exactly what it feels like to be in the wilderness, tempted and challenged by the devil. I come to You as my great High Priest, the One who can sympathize with my weakness, trusting that You will help me in this my time of need.

    a. Please equip me to use Your Word of fire to strengthen my feeble heart;

    b. I will trust in You and I give You all of the glory, Amen!

13. Lord God, in **Psalm 144:10,** You were the One who gave victory to Your servant, King David. You freed him from the

deadly swords. Make each of the following prayers in the name of Jesus Christ:

    a. I shall emerge victorious in this spiritual battle;

    b. I recover all what the tyrants have held captive in my life;

    c. *"I shall not die, but I shall live, and recount the deeds of the Lord"* (Psalm 118:17).

14. Arrow of satanic judgment that is assigned by day/night, backfire, in the name of Jesus Christ.

15. O Lord Jesus Christ, let not the hand of the wicked remove me. Let them be cast down and *"never to rise again"* (Amos 5:2), in the name of Jesus Christ.

16. As from now on, all those who want to devour me shall be devoured and preyed upon (Jeremiah 30:16), in the name of Jesus Christ.

17. Thank You, Lord Jesus Christ, for using this prayer to return fire for fire for my sake.

    a. *"But thanks be to God, who gives us the victory through our Lord Jesus Christ"* (1 Corinthians 15:57).

    b. Offer songs of thanksgiving.

18. I cover this prayer with the Most Precious Blood of Jesus Christ (7 times).

Chapter 8

OPERATION OVERTAKE
THE TYRANTS

· ◦ ◆ ◆ ◆ ◆ ◦ ·

*"David inquired of the Lord, "Shall I pursue this band?
Shall I overtake them?" He answered him, "Pursue;
for you shall surely overtake and shall surely rescue...
David attacked them from twilight until the evening
of the next day. Not one of them escaped, except four
hundred young men, who mounted camels and fled.
David recovered all that the Amalekites had taken; and
David rescued his two wives. Nothing was missing,
whether small or great, sons or daughters, spoil or
anything that had been taken; David brought back
everything."*

(I Samuel 30:8, 17-19)

(Other suggested Bible passages to read:
I Samuel 30: 1-31, Exodus 14:1-31, Exodus 15:1-21,
Genesis 31:22-55, Psalm 18:1-50, I Samuel 17:1-58,
2 Chronicles 20:1-29, I Kings 18:1-45).

DAY 16
Part 1: Reflection

Some years ago, a professor friend of mine, while in a dream,
saw himself being chased by some wild dogs. It was a hot chase!
The dogs caught him and gave him severe bites. Deep were

the wounds he suffered in the dream. Upon waking up from sleep in the morning, he shared the dream with his wife but concluded that the dream was a sign that he has some malaria parasites in his blood. He concluded that it was a symptom of malaria because of the assertion that people who suffer from malaria may experience some weird dreams. My professor friend, a gentleman, went by the books—what else would you expect from a "Prof"?—but he got it all wrong! Although he goes to Church and holds a high position in his Parish, yet he does not understand spiritual matters. Spiritual matters require a revelation knowledge, not empirical knowledge!

That morning, at school, the professor's wife called my attention to her office and narrated her husband's dream to me. She wanted to know if there's any need for concern. I explained to her the dream and alerted her to tell Prof. that his enemy has overtaken him and that he urgently needed to get into serious prayers to abort it. Prof. didn't pay any attention to this—he wondered the correlation between his dream and prayers. And because he could not see a correlation between the two, he swept the need for prayer under the carpet.

I needed not to be told that Prof. is not well educated in spiritual matters. I could imagine him saying, "Well, if it is not scientifically proven, then it is a superstition." He went for the Doctor's prescription for treatment of malaria. Hmmm, at this point, I can't help but reflect on the words of Festus to Paul: *"You are out of your mind, Paul! Too much learning is driving you insane!"* (Acts 26:24)—only that "Paul" shall be replaced with "Prof."

The result of his ignorance played out that same week as a group of armed robbers raided his family on the weekend. He cannot forget the terrible panic he went through. Upon hearing the seemingly never-ending shootings in the midnight and seeing the number of armed robbers approaching his house on looking through his window, he simply opened the window of his upstairs and jumped out into a thick forest on pajamas, not minding the height of fall and possible weapons he might fall upon. He narrated how he spent the whole night in the frigid weather under heavy downpour and without proper clothing (remember, all what he had on was a pair of pajamas on a frosty weather). He lost a fortune that night to his enemies (the armed robbers).

Prof. could have averted this situation had he had spiritual understanding of his dream that God was revealing to him an impending danger. Oh, poor Prof.! What a price you have to pay for your ignorance!

The wild dogs that bite Prof. in the dream represent the enemy— in this case, the armed robbers— that came and attacked him. Evidently, my professor friend was overtaken by his enemies (as represented by the dogs chasing him, getting to him and launching bites). He lost the battle in the spirit, and it played out in the physical. It is high time we realize that the physical events in life are controlled from the spiritual realm—this is true even when we are ignorant of it, like Prof!

However, having spiritual knowledge and using the power of prayer can abort every diabolical spiritual operation against us.

In the Chapter 9 of Volume 1 of this book, we learned of a prayerful lady who, upon receiving in her dream a letter with the lone word CANCER written on it, chose to go into serious prayers so as to abort the plan of the enemy to afflict her with cancer just like her sister who died of cancer. She did not suffer the cancer in the physical realm because she had spiritually intercepted the spirit sent to afflict her with cancer. As for my friend "Prof.", instead of intercepting the enemy's plot against him, his ignorance played out as the enemy had a free day to implement their orchestrated debauchery. Scripture says, *"My people are destroyed for lack of knowledge; because you have rejected knowledge, I reject you from being a priest to me"* (Hosea 4:6). If we reject the knowledge of what God says about the kingdom of darkness, how can we stand strong against the enemy?

The word "overtake" may be defined as being able to catch up with or to pass after catching up with. It could also mean to come upon someone or something unexpectedly and as such take such a thing or one by surprise. For sure, we see the meaning of "overtake" played out in Prof.'s story as he was overtaken by his enemies.

We also see the power to overtake in **I Samuel 16:1-13** as the little boy David—seemingly forgotten by his father, Jesse, and siblings (when Samuel came to anoint the next king of Israel)—was anointed in front of his seven brothers as the new King of Israel. Although David was not in the parade when Prophet Samuel visited, yet he was the head upon whom the oil of anointing rested. David, the least among his brothers, became the first in Israel—putting his brothers under him. David had overtaken his brother and even overtook all the soldiers of Israel that would have normally hushed him up!

Yet, we see another heart-rending story of the power to overtake in **Exodus 14** as the Israelites crossed the Red Sea disadvantaging the Egyptians. In order to force the Israelites back into captivity, Pharaoh's soldiers tried to overtake them as the Israelites made their escape. We see the hopelessness of the Israelites as the Egyptian armies were angrily approaching the Israelites who were blocked by the Red Sea. It was clear that the Egyptians would overtake the Israelites. God took over this hopeless situation and made the Israelites to cross over the Red Sea which drowned the Egyptians as they were attempting to cross over the sea. Evidently, the Israelites overtook the Egyptians as they watched their enemies drowned in the sea. The hand of God made the Israelites to overtake the Egyptians as He turned the Red Sea into a powerful weapon to permanently defeat the Egyptians.

The Bible tells us that Satan comes to kill, steal, and to destroy **(John 10:10)**. However, before Satan kills, steals, or destroys someone, he must have overpowered, overcome or overtaken the person. On this note, the scripture says, *"When a strong man, fully armed, guards his own palace, his goods are in peace. But when a stronger than he comes upon him and overcomes him, he takes from him all his armor in which he trusted, and divides his spoils"* **(Luke 11:21-22, NKJV)**. It is after Satan and his demons have overtaken us that they proceed *"to steal"* our blessings from us with the obvious intentions to kill what they have just stolen from us.

We can go through anything in life as long as the situation or the storm does not overtake us. Be reminded that any ship can make it through any storm, but not when overtaken by it. Wisdom demands that we should not allow the enemy to overtake us. Rather, we should overtake and destroy the enemy lest they overtake us.

The Philistines laid in wait all night against Samson hoping to overtake him in order to kill him with an ambush attack in the morning, but Samson overtook them by waking up in the midnight (that is before light of the morning) and took hold of the doors of the enemy's city, pulling it down **(Judges 16:2-3)**. Samson fought offensively, and not defensively— the best defense is a good offense, people say! We should not allow the devil and his companions to overtake us, and steal from us.

In the physical world, there are certain unique jobs, duties, and specialties that the soldiers have—one soldier may be a pulling-down expert while another one may be a communication expert. It is the same in the spiritual world: some demonic spirits may specialize in greed, with assignments to cause people to never be satisfied with what they have. Another demon may be a demon of anger, whose purpose is to keep a person locked in a vicious cycle of lifelong anger. While another demon may specialize in near-success syndrome, causing people to miscarry their blessings at the edge of a breakthrough. These spirits find a safe haven to operate and overtake folks when people are living in ignorance of the way things work in the world.

My dear, I don't know what the tyrants have stolen from your life but with God on your side, you shall live to tell your survival story. The ultimate insurance against the tyrant's mission to sink your destiny with life's storms is to have God on your side. Could God be whispering to you that it is time to recover all that the tyrants have plundered in your life? Yes, you shall recover all, in the name of Jesus Christ! David recovered all; and so shall you.

In **1 Samuel 30,** King David and his men arrived at the city of Ziklag, only to find out that tyrants had attacked them from behind while at war fighting another tyrant. The Amalekites had burned down the entire city. And yet, as if this was not enough, the Amalekites took captive King David's wives as well as the wives and children of his men. Sometimes tyrants come from different directions to swamp a child of God with troubles. Yesterday, it was a divorce court case, debts and hospital bills to settle; today, it is sickness and an accident, while the mailbox still holds a letter of unpaid insurance and threat letter from an ex-husband/ex-wife. Tyrant spirits have expertise in dumping entire truck load of sorrows on people.

However, David strengthened himself in the Lord, who assured him that he would overtake the enemy, and would recover all. With God on his side, David recovered all. Nothing was missing. The Word of God assures us that *"The steps of a good man are ordered by the LORD, and He delights in his way. Though he falls, he shall not be utterly cast down; For the LORD upholds him with His hand"* (Psalm 37:23-24, NKJV). My dear, it is time for you to overtake the enemy and rightfully recover all your possessions that have been taken captive by the tyrants! Never dare to forfeit what is rightfully yours. Our Christ has given us authority to repossess our possessions that are seized by the tyrants. Child of God, you are guaranteed full recovery of your children who are kidnapped by the enemies. Time has come for us to pray to recover our spouses, family members and loved ones who are taken captive by the enemy.

The enemies are battle ready to outwit you and confiscate your blessings but it is high time you change your prayer pattern and strategy to recover all that they took away. They won't succumb until you weary them with an unceasing bombardment of acidic prayers. You must fight to overtake your enemies before you can reach for your bumper harvest! This is what this chapter invites you to do. Whether there are spirits or situations that have been overtaking you, you are going to cry out to God to make you an overtaker of them that have been overtaking you.

It was after Elijah prayed that Ahab rode away on a horse to escape the heavy rain, but *"the power of the Lord came on Elijah... and [he] ran ahead of Ahab all the way to Jezreel* (1 Kings 18:46, GNT). In the name of Jesus Christ, I pray for you that the hands of the Lord shall lift you up, drop you in the front and cause you to remain there up till the end of the 'race'.

LET US PRAY!

1. Reflect on how this reflection on "Operation Overtake the Tyrants" ministers to you.

2. Pray the Saint Michael the Archangel prayer (see page 17).

3. Pray the Anima Christi prayer (see page 18).

4. Pray Psalm 7 (a prayer to overtake the enemy).

5. *"I pursued my enemies and overtook them; and did not turn back until they were consumed"* (Psalm 18:37)—I pray in the name of Jesus Christ.

6. I decree that now is the time for my possessions held captive in the North, South, East, and West to come to me —in the name of Jesus Christ (Pray very hard for at least 2 minutes!).

7. Begin to release some arrows of fire to every spiritual operation on a mission to overtake you. End each prayer point with "in the name of Jesus Christ, Amen!"

   a. I release sharp arrows of fire into the hearts of the tyrants that are chasing me **(Psalm 45:5)**;

   b. My *"tongue is a deadly arrow"* **(Jeremiah 9:8)**. Therefore, I release it to scatter the enemies that are after me and my loved ones. **(Psalm 18:14)**;

   c. My tongue is like *"a bronze arrow [that] will strike them through"* **(Job 20:24)**. Therefore, I release it to strike through the enemies that want to overtake me and my family;

   d. With the hands of the Lord upon me, I shoot out my *"arrows and destroy"* the enemies **(Psalm 144:6)**;

   e. *"But God will shoot his arrow at them; they will be wounded suddenly"* **(Psalm 64:7)**. Therefore, I set aside and allow God to get into my battlefield and fight all of the tyrants that want to overtake me and my household;

   f. O Lord, let Your *"arrow go forth like lightning"* **(Zechariah 9:14)** as *"Your arrows flashed on every side"* to pin down the enemies **(Psalm 77:17)**;

8. Begin to make the following commands in the name of Jesus Christ. In the name of Jesus Christ:

    a. I command the devil to take his head, hands and legs off my finances;

    b. I command every demonic vehicle loading and transporting away my blessings to be grounded forever;

    c. I command *"the wheels of their chariots"* to jam, which are fighting to overtake me **(Exodus 14:25, NIV)**;

    d. Let every robber of my blessing be rendered null and void;

    e. I command all my benefits that are captured by spiritual robbers in the dream to become too hot for them to handle;

    f. I command my lost glory to come back to me;

    g. I command the grave to bring up whatever it is holding that belongs to me.

9. Begin to make the following decrees in the name of Jesus Christ. In the name of Jesus Christ:

    a. I decree a seven-fold restoration of everything that spiritual thieves have stolen from me;

    b. I decree that my blessings shall be too hot for the enemy to sit upon;

    c. I decree that this prayer shall catapult me to my next level;

    d. I decree that greater harvest of miracles shall begin in my life from today;

    e. I decree that my spiritual power and anointing shall be restored through this prayer.

10. Thank the Lord and cover this prayer with the Most Precious Blood of Jesus Christ (7 times).

DAY 17

Part 2: Warfare Prayers

Note:

- Be very aggressive in this prayer! You want to overtake, not to be overtaken!!

1. Offer God some Spirit-filled praise and/or worship songs as the Spirit leads.

2. Pray **Psalm 51** for repentance and forgiveness of sins.
   a. Confess and renounce your sins;
   b. I repent and receive forgiveness for any sin that has opened the door for any evil spirit to enter and operate in my life, family, ministry or Church, in the name of Jesus Christ **(Ephesians 4:27)**.

3. Pray the prayer of Saint Michael the Archangel (see page 17).

4. Pray the Anima Christi prayer (see page 18).

5. I cover myself and my household, and the environment of this prayer with the Most Precious Blood of Jesus Christ (7 times).

6. Lord Jesus, I ask You for the divine strength to pursue and overtake my enemies—and recover all my blessings from them—in the name of Jesus Christ.

7. *"Judah has gone into exile with suffering...her pursuers have all overtaken her in the midst of her distress"* (Lamentations 1:3).

   a. I decree that those pursuing me shall not overtake me—not even *"in the midst of distress"*—in the name of Jesus Christ;

b. My enemies shall not rejoice over me, in the name of Jesus Christ;

c. All tyrants that want to chase me "into exile with suffering", I command all of the sufferings you wished on me to be eternally glued to you and I drive you all immediately into annihilating exile—in the name of Jesus Christ.

8. Holy Spirit, help me to be well educated in spiritual matters, in the name of Jesus Christ. Make the following prayers, in the name of Jesus Christ:

a. Lord Jesus, help me to see my errors that enable the enemy to steal from me;

b. Lord Jesus, help me to yield wholly to the disciplines of the Holy Spirit;

c. Lord Jesus, help me with the grace to do all in my power to overcome desires to live ungodly life.

9. Through this prayer, I intercept every orchestrated diabolical spiritual operation that has been set in motion against me, in the name of Jesus Christ.

10. 1 **Samuel 30:19** says that *"nothing was missing."* David recovered all that were stolen from him and his people. Therefore, in the name of Jesus Christ:

a. I recover all that the devil and his demon spirits took away from me (for example, your career, finances, prayer life, glory, crowns, and so on);

b. The Amalekites had managed to "*steal*" and carry away every man, woman, and child from David's camp (**1 Samuel 30:3**). Use this opportunity to pray so as to recover your marriage, family members, loved ones, relationships which were taken captive by the enemy.

    c. I take a count of my family (and our blessings) *"and not one of us is missing"* (**Numbers 31:49**):
        i. And so shall it be forever in my lineage;
       ii. We shall count upwards, not downwards.
      iii. We shall get stronger and stronger, not weaker and weaker (**2 Samuel 3:1**).
    d. With authority, I repossess all my possessions that have been seized by the tyrants.

11. I shall not miss my time of divine appointment —in the name of Jesus Christ (Pray very hard for at least 2 minutes!).

12. I decree that every throne that is preventing me from seeing my God-given destiny fulfilled must be dismantled right now through this prayer—in the name of Jesus Christ (Pray very hard for at least 2 minutes!).

13. Anything in my foundation that is assigned to prevent me from reaching my goals in life, be destroyed by fire right now—in the name of Jesus Christ (Pray very hard for at least 2 minutes!).

14. In the name of Jesus Christ, I rebuke every power that is humiliating me, contending with my destiny, and holding me down. Your time is up, in the name of Jesus Christ! (Pray very hard for at least 2 minutes!).

15. Holy Spirit, help me to come up with a spirit-led plan of recovery to keep me at the top, beyond the reach of the enemy.

16. I receive the anointing to overtake my overtakers, in the name of Jesus Christ.

17. I receive the anointing for divine speed over my enemies, in the name of Jesus Christ.

18. I receive the anointing to be the head and not the tail, in the name of Jesus Christ.

19. I receive the anointing to come out of every hopeless situation, in the name of Jesus Christ.

20. I receive the anointing to win every spiritual battle, in the name of Jesus Christ.

21. In the name of Jesus Christ, my enemy shall not succeed in giving me a surprised attack.

22. In the name of Jesus Christ, I block the spiritual enemies chasing me.

23. I paralyze, with the stones of fire, every spirit of Goliath that is holding my divine elevation, in the name of Jesus Christ.

24. Every ordinance that is causing me to be overtaken by the enemies (and to lag behind in life), be broken, in the name of Jesus Christ.

25. *"All these blessings shall come upon you and overtake you, if you obey the Lord your God"* (Deuteronomy 28:2). Begin to pronounce blessings upon yourself that you desire to see overtake you (you may choose to stand before the mirror and bless yourself in the mirror).

26. Pray in the Spirit for at least five minutes.

27. Begin to thank the Lord for your victory through this prayer.
    a. Thank you, Lord Jesus Christ, for answering my prayers

and empowering me to recover all that I were stolen from me;

b. Thank God with Praise and worship for what He has done for You through this prayer;

c. Pray **Psalm 47** and **Psalm 48.**

28. I cover this prayer with the Most Precious Blood of Jesus Christ (7 times).

Chapter 9
DIVINE DELIVERANCE

· · ✦ ◆ ✦ · ·

"Little children, you are from God, and have conquered them; for the one who is in you is greater than the one who is in the world"

(1 John 4:4)

"The God of peace will shortly crush Satan under your feet. The grace of our Lord Jesus Christ be with you."

(Romans 16:20)

(Other suggested Bible passages to read:
Isaiah 43:18-19, Psalm 91, Romans 6:14-19,
1 Corinthians 15:55-58, Ephesians 6:10-18, 2 Kings 11).

DAY 18
Part 1: Reflection

Have you ever made a piece of toast, slathered it with butter and strawberry jam, and just as you were about to take the first delicious bite, something unexpected happened and it dropped on the floor? I'm embarrassed to admit that this has happened to me. While this incident is an accident, a pattern of such an event is not an accident! For example, it is an accident for you to trip on a stone and fall, but it is no more an accident if this keep happening only when something good is about to come into your life. Why would your well always run dry only when you are thirsty and need some water to drink? Why would every promise to you end up unfulfilled?—I don't mean the unfulfilled campaigns promises of the politicians, but personal promises made on the platter of certainty. How many "motherhood-statements" or promises have ended up in miscarriages? Hmmm! I can't help but think of the mirage on a hot and sunny day that is promising a pool of refreshing waters that never comes true. I recall the deep sobbing of a sister whose intelligence at class promises that she would pass her licensing exam with flying colors but to the surprise of everyone—including herself—she keeps failing the exam from year to year notwithstanding all the efforts that she puts into it. The disturbing thing in her situation was that each time she entered the exam room and was ready to write, a certain overpowering heaviness descended on her at that moment, so strong that she would sleep in the exam room only to return to reality at the end of the examination time period when it was too late for her to complete the exam. Again—this is not an accident!

If this is also your own story, then I crave for the effrontery to look into your eye balls and tell you that I see myself in your eyes. I already admitted to everyone that my piece of toast accidently dropped on the floor when my salivating mouth was ready for the first delicious bite. My friend, I want to admit here that everything in the first paragraph of this chapter was my story—well, with the exception that I never slept in the exam hall! It wasn't only my toast that dropped off my hand when I was ready for a lunch, but every good thing was dropping off from me to the floor. Like a tree shedding her leaves in the autumn season, I seemed to be in the autumn of my life as the splendor of my life was dropping like autumn leaves. I became a picture of hopelessness, to say the least! From the very *"wells of salvation*" that others were joyfully drawing their water **(Isaiah 12:3)**, I met empty cisterns with mud **(Jeremiah 38:6)**! It seemed as if I was fetching mud of shame where people fetched their refreshing waters. Mine was so patterned to the point that a friend once made a joke to me saying, "*O Boy, I have noticed in your life that hell breaks loose when a good thing is about to reach your hands.*" He was correct! I knew.

Oh, I just remember something to whisper into your ear: Did you hear me ask in the first paragraph, "*Why would your well always run dry only when you are thirsty and need some water to drink?*" Let me tell you where that question first came from before making it to the pages of this book. It was the very question that I asked myself several times when I was neck-deep with life problems. Every promise from people literally developed wings and flew "*like a bird to the mountains*" **(Psalm 11:1)**. Friends in positions to help failed me—this one was a bitter pill to chew because we were too close in our university days. I probably suffered more miscarriages than any woman could "boast" of miscarrying her baby. Believe me!

Now, if I may ask you, drop this book by your side for a moment, please. Don't do any other thing. Relax a little bit. Close your eyes for a minute or two. Now, think of why God brought this book your way. An accident? No! God chose to speak to you with this book! This book has a voice. I would jokingly say that a spiritual dissection of this book reveals the power of God's voice and the light of His Presence running through some invisible arteries of every sentence of this book—all to bring enlightenment to you.

God is speaking to you using this book, my friend! He brought this book to you because He wants to deliver you from the invisible enemies that are attacking your life. So, brighten up! Tell the devil that you "*shall not die, but... shall live, and recount the deeds of the Lord*" **(Psalm 118:17). Pray Psalm 23** and meditate on it.

We live in a world where people trust products by the testimonies of those who have used the product and certified its trustworthiness. If you are not sure of the testimony of Abraham or Jabez because you don't know them, then I am that testimony that you need in order to believe that God can deliver a man from the most terrible situation of his or her life. We probably would have been "partners in suffering" now—who knows—had God not intervened to change my story; but even then, God changed my story so that I would be a living testimony that confirms to you that your own vindication is on the way. Yes, your testimony is coming! I can assure you that my toasts don't fall off my hands anymore! In fact, now, toasts look for my hands! And soon, my friend, we shall be "partners in praise", praising God for delivering us! *"Wait for it; it will certainly come and will not delay"* (Habakkuk 2:3).

A tyrant will make sure that you don't have your blessings, and not to talk of enjoying them. I once encountered a bizarre case in which an unseen hand repeatedly knocked food out from the hand of a certain man whenever he was about to put the food into his mouth. Imagine all the efforts spent before food comes to the table, only for the spiritual tyrant to wait for him at the table so as to stop him from enjoying the labor of his hands.

As I write this chapter, I recall this man's ordeal: I recall the times that this spirit stopped him from being a free man! A tyrant spirit will fight you to make sure that you don't take a delicious bite after your labor. He wants you to build houses but never inhabit them; he also wants you to plant vineyards but never eat their fruits. He wants you to bear children for calamity (Isaiah 65:23). They are satisfied if your food is in the dust! The tyrant wants to see you suffer and live in shame, and never live your dreams. Is this the picture of your life? If so, then you need deliverance. I mean divine deliverance!

The *Webster Dictionary* defines "Deliverance" as, *"To set free or liberate; to release or save."* The tyrant is a spiritual force that does not want us to be free or liberated. Thus, in praying with Jesus Christ in the prayer that He Himself taught us, it is fitting to ask God to *"Rescue us from the evil one"* **(Matthew 6:13)**—a prayer of plea for protection that reveals our need to be freed or saved from the devil and his co-tyrants. It is important that we have victory over every tyrant force.

You may ask: "But what should I do when the tyrant turns against me?" The answer is that you MUST run to God to deliver you from the raging tyrant. Draw strength from God by putting Him into the equation and trusting solely in Him. God never refused to bring His deliverance to those who earnestly sought for it. He delivers those who put their hope and trust in Him. He delivers them from wolves and lions who try prey upon them. My dear, God is on a rescue mission now and every day—a mission to deliver you from every dangerous terrain and raging storm. He comes to lift the weight of hopelessness from us so that we will have a good and glorious ending.

When we meet Naomi in the Scriptures, we see the wreck that the spiritual tyrants caused in her life **(Ruth 1)**. Life was going well with her family when, all of a sudden, her husband and her two sons died (in a short space of time) in a foreign land. Her toast dropped when she was ready to eat it. In an age where men were the sole providers for their families and sons were a badge of honor to a woman, this was not a small problem for Naomi. This is not a pretty picture at all! She was knocked down and paralyzed by the spiritual tyrants of Moab[1] . Naomi's pain was heartbreaking, and her wounds were as *"deep as the sea"* **(Lamentations 2:13, NIV).** A tyrant attacks everything that God has given to us. Remember the case of Job in which the devil attacked everything he had.

---

1. Spiritual tyrants can anesthetize, knock down, brainwash and spiritually paralyze someone.

Yet, in the end, God proved His capability to deliver Naomi from the ugly situation that befell her. In responding to the situation of the destitute and broken Naomi, God did not only wipe her tears using Boaz, *"a kinsman-redeemer"* (**Ruth 4:14, BSB**), but also through her daughter-in-law, Ruth, God wiped away the tears of the entire mankind as she became an ancestress of Jesus Christ, *"the Redeemer of mankind"* (**Matthew 1:5**). Naomi did not know that God was positioning her to be greatly used to bring deliverance to the entire world—and that for this purpose, she was sent to Moab to bring just a woman (Ruth) to Bethlehem whom He will use!

Has it ever crossed your mind that cooperating with God in the hopeless situation that you are going through now will bring the deliverance of many in a time that is yet to come? In Naomi's excruciating pain, God was at work. So was God at work in Joseph's troubles that came to him through his brothers...and so shall He be for you! He's at work in your life even when you're not aware of it. So, don't give up: Divine Deliverance is coming to you!

If there seems to be no way out of your despair now, remember that Naomi's God is your God as well. He is a specialist in delivering His people from every *"horrible pit"* in which they find themselves and will set their *"feet upon a rock"* (**Psalm 40:2, NKJV**). Therefore, in the midst of your daily challenges, contradictions, temptations and adversities, be rest-assured that your God is both capable to deliver you *and* faithful to do so to bring glory to Himself. Always remember that God is the manager of all that plays out in our lives. He never allows our faithfulness to go unrewarded. His unseen hand is working out praise out of that mess—as **Romans 8:28** assures us: *"We know that all things work together for good for those who love God, who are called according to His purpose."* Therefore, when the tyrant messes with you, remember who your God is!

Do you really believe that God is doing something even when things take an unexpected turn, relationships fail, finances falter, or the doctor calls back with grim news? My dear, God is still the Manager when He lets trials shake your world! Remember that He is always in control, if you allow Him. Jesus Christ is the best security against the disaster and destructions that are perpetuated by spiritual tyrants. He is the only foundation that can keep us safe. In Him, we do not need to fear our adversaries. Is the Lord Jesus Christ *"the sure foundation"* of your life **(Isaiah 28:16)**?

We must, therefore, engage the tyrant entities in a spiritual warfare using God's weapons of warfare to bring down the tyrants, destroy their strongholds, and recover our stolen blessings. That is the pathway to our freedom and deliverance from the tyrant's choking grip. Always remember that we are *"more than conquerors"* in Christ **(Romans 8:37)**. Spiritual fighters get what they want— Deliverance! Victory! Dominion! The kingdom of God suffers violence (Matthew 11:12) when we sit on the sidelines rather than engage in battle.

LET US PRAY!

1. Reflect on how this reflection on "Divine Deliverance" ministers to you.

2. Pray the Saint Michael the Archangel prayer (see page 17).

3. Pray the Anima Christi prayer (see page 18).

4. Pray **Psalm 140** (a prayer of deliverance from evil plots).

5. In the name of Jesus Christ, I release----- (*pick from the following list*) against the spiritual forces that are fighting me and all of my loved ones.

  - *"Engines of war"* (**Ezekiel 26:9, KJV**)
  - *"Instruments of death"* (**Psalm 7:13, KJV**)
  - *"Instruments of war"* (**1 Samuel 8:12, KJV**)
  - A swallowing earth (**Numbers 16:28-33**)
  - Fear of the day and night (**Deuteronomy 28:66**)
  - Thunder of God (**2 Samuel 22:14**)
  - *"Whirlwind and tempest"* (**Isaiah 29:6c**)
  - Destroying earthquake (**Revelation 11:13**)
  - The drowning "Red Sea" (**Exodus 14:26-28**)
  - Hail & fire (**Exodus 9:13-35**)
  - *"A stream of fire"* (**Daniel 7:10**)
  - The Fire of death (**Numbers 11:2**)
  - *"Flames of devouring fire"* (**Isaiah 29:6d**)
  - Paralyzing fear (**2 Chronicles 20:29**)
  - The spirit of deep sleep (**Isaiah 29:10**)
  - The drowning "Red Sea" (**Exodus 14:26-28**)
  - Boils and rashes (**Exodus 9:8-12**)
  - The "blast of God" (**Job 4:9, KJV**)
  - *"War-horses"* (**Joel 2:4**)
  - Devouring locusts (**Exodus 10:1-15**)
  - God's judgment (**Isaiah 24:21**)
  - Divine punishment (**Isaiah 24:21**)
  - Confusion (**2 Chronicles 20:22**)

6. In the name of Jesus Christ, let their ----- (*pick from the following list*).
  - Hands turn leprous (**Exodus 4:6**)
  - Rivers be plagued (**Exodus 7:14-25**)
  - Lands be plagued with killing flies (**Exodus 8:20-24**)
  - Lands be plagued with spiritual diseases (**Exodus 9:1-7**)
  - Lands turn into thick and blinding darkness (**Exodus 10:21-23**)

- "Rods" of power be swallowed up by my prayer (**Exodus 7:12**)
- "Snakes" swallow themselves up.

7. Pray against patterns that come up in your life as an accident when you are about to eat your "buttered toast". O Lord Jesus, I tap into Your promise that says: *"In vain you rise early and stay up late, toiling for food to eat— for he grants sleep to those he loves"* (**Psalm 127:2**). Therefore, in the name of Jesus Christ, I decree that...

    a. Never again shall I work like an elephant but eat like an ant;

    b. Never again shall my "buttered bread" (blessings) slip out of my hands;

    c. I *"shall not plant and another eat"* (Isaiah 65:22);

    d. I *"shall not labor in vain"* (Isaiah 65:23a);

    e. I *"shall not... bear children for calamity"* (Isaiah 65:23b);

    f. *"All my wicked neighbors who seize the inheritance"* that God has given to me shall be uprooted from my land (**Jeremiah 12:14 NIV**);

    g. Every trend of inability to hold on to a job be broken now (pray very hard!)

    h. This year, ----- (*pick from the following list*) shall fulfill its purpose, in the name of Jesus Christ.

    - My destiny
    - My efforts
    - My marriage
    - My life
    - My prayers
    - My plans

8. Pray against evil family patterns of aborted testimonies and blessings. In the name of Jesus Christ, I pray that ...

    a. Evil foundations of near-success syndrome in my life shall be destroyed now!

    b. Everything in my foundation that is standing between me and my promised land be uprooted;

    c. From now onwards, no other foundation is permitted to stand in my life, except the foundation of Jesus Christ;

    d. Every satanic foundation in my family line be set on fire!

    e. I delete out of my life every evil handwriting of failure and stagnancy at work in me;

    f. I rebel against where the enemy has kept me;

    g. Every altar of premature death in my bloodline be destroyed now (pray very hard!).

9. Thank the Lord and cover this prayer with the Most Precious Blood of Jesus Christ (7 times).

DAY 19

Part 2: Warfare Prayers

Note:

- The best deliverance is achieved when we sincerely repent of our sinful ways and then seek to live a life of holiness and prayerfulness.

- Deliverance will give you freedom, and spiritual warfare will give you the training and strategies to the freedom that you seek.

- Let the strength of your bows of prayer carry your arrows of deliverance to the galls of the tyrants, piercing them with accurate blows of force.

1. Praise and worship God as the Holy Spirit directs you. Father in heaven, I come before You in the mighty name of Jesus Christ. I praise You, Lord Jesus Christ:

    a. For Your power and great glory;

    b. For You are *"The Lord, strong and mighty, the Lord, mighty in battle"* **(Psalm 24:8);**

    c. For You are *"my fortress, and my deliverer, my God, my rock in whom I take refuge, my shield, and the horn of my salvation, my stronghold"* (Psalm 18:2);

d. For You *"brought them out of darkness and the shadow of death, and broke their chains in pieces. Oh, that men would give thanks to the Lord for His goodness, and for His wonderful works to the children of men! For He has broken the gates of bronze, and cut the bars of iron in two"* (Psalm 107:14-16, NKJV).

2. Use **Psalm 51** to ask God for the forgiveness of your sins.

   a. Lord Jesus Christ, help me to realize whatever displeases You in my life and grant me the grace to make amends—I am sorry, Lord;

   b. Lord Jesus Christ, help me to realize how I have given spiritual tyrants access into my life (ask for the grace to deal with it appropriately as the Holy Spirit brings them to the surface)—I am sorry, Lord;

   c. Holy Spirit, please show me any unconfessed sin that the enemy is holding on to in order to limit the efficacy of this prayer—I am sorry, Lord;

   d. Lord Holy Spirit, show me anyone who needs my forgiveness, and grant me the grace to forgive them from my heart (forgive them);

   e. Lord Jesus Christ, I thank You for forgiving me my sins.

3. Pray the prayer of Saint Michael the Archangel (see page 17).

4. Pray the Anima Christi prayer (see page 18).

5. Dress up for war and fight! Make every prayer aggressively and "in the name of Jesus Christ":

   a. I suit up with the whole armor of God **(Ephesians 6:14-17)**:

      i. I put on the helmet of salvation, the breastplate of

righteousness, the belt of truth, and my feet is shod with the gospel of peace;

ii. I take up the shield of faith, which quenches every fiery dart of the wicked one and the sword of the Spirit which is the Word of God;

iii. I take up the garments of vengeance and the cloak of zeal **(Isaiah 59:17);**

iv. I surround myself with divine smoke screen **(Exodus 19:18)** acting as a sight and sound barrier against satanic agents, interlopers, and evil spirits;

b. I release the Blood of Jesus Christ against all evil spirits and satanic agents that have taken up assignments against my home, family, business, economy, and my prayer life:

c. I decree that the weapons of my warfare are not carnal but mighty in God to the tearing down of strongholds, the casting down of arguments and of every high thing which exalts itself against the knowledge of Christ **(2 Corinthians 10:4).**

6. I command all escape routes of the enemies to be shut down right now, in the name of Jesus Christ.

7. I overtake the enemies that are fleeing, stabbing them to death with my sword of fire, in the name of Jesus Christ.

8. I declare a spiritual clearance in the spiritual atmosphere of my life and the lives of those connected to me, in the name of Jesus Christ.

9. With the armies of God's Angels by my side, I release a carnage against the enemy that has surrounded me, persecuted me, opposed me, and resisted me—in the name of Jesus Christ.

10. To the kingdom of darkness, I release arrows, lightning,

hailstones, tornadoes, tsunamis, volcanoes, lava and an avalanche of coals of fire—in the name of Jesus Christ.

11. In the name of Jesus Christ, I scatter the enemies that have gathered themselves against me with famine **(Ezekiel 5:16)** and devouring storms **(Psalm 83:15-17)**.

12. In the name of Jesus Christ, I decree that all armies of the satanic kingdom that are fighting me shall be drowned in the Sea of Death.

13. Lord Jesus Christ, please empower me to always take the steps of faith against spiritual tyrants and every horde of demonic forces by acting on Your promises, no matter how hopeless things might appear to be—I pray in the name of Jesus Christ.

14. Lord Jesus Christ, grant me the faith that does not see problems but sees Your hands working out victory for me—in the name of Jesus Christ.

15. Take this prayer seriously. According to **Jude 1:23,** "Snatch others from the fire and save them." Plead with God to deliver other people who are enslaved by the evil one.
    a. Pray for unbelievers as the Holy Spirit leads you;
    b. I plead with You, Lord Jesus Christ, to deliver Your people from every spirit of ----- (say, "In the name of Jesus Christ" after each prayer point).

- Sadness and obsessions
- Hatred, fornication, envy
- Sinful sexuality
- Harmful friendship
- The occult
- Evil manipulation

- Thoughts of suicide and abortion
- Thoughts of jealousy, rage, and death
- Division in our family
- Spell and witchcraft
- Living in error
- Backwardness

16. By the power in the name of Jesus Christ, I banish from my life and family, all manners of fellowship with the devil.

17. Pray against life of living in errors that hinder your progress. Ask God for forgiveness for indulging in living such a life. In the name of Jesus Christ, I command ...
    a. Every negative attitude that I have carried along for years to be eradicated now (pray very hard!);
    b. Every ungodly addiction in my life to be broken now (pray very hard!);
    c. Instant termination of all evil activities that hinder my success;
    d. You troubler of my life to fall and never rise again;
    e. The spirits that stir up problems at the nick of my breakthrough to catch fire;
    f. My feet to carry me to places of blessings and to never fail me;
    g. My feet not to take me to where there are troubles and disasters;
    h. Every horn of ----- (*pick from the following list*) in my life must be broken now, in the name of Jesus Christ.

    - Wickedness
    - Poverty
    - Disaster
    - Laziness
    - Affliction
    - Mistakes
    - Infirmity
    - Vagabond
    - Backwardness
    - Stagnation
    - Disfavor
    - Hard luck

18. O Lord Jesus Christ, fulfill in my life Your Word in **Psalm 107:14** which says , *"He brought them out of darkness and the shadow of death, and broke their chains in pieces"* (NIV)—in the name of Jesus Christ. Therefore, in the name of Jesus Christ I decree:
    a. That this year, I shall lift up my head in promotion!
    b. That from today, I will begin to prosper wherever I have previously failed;

    c. That my health and my strength shall not fail me;

    d. That as the grave could not hold Jesus Christ, so shall no grave hold my deliverance.

19. I command spiritual locusts **(Exodus 10:1-20)** and ravenous birds **(Ezekiel 39:4)** to devour the evil words and curses that are spoken against me, my household, destiny, business, divine calling and everything under my stewardship—in the name of Jesus Christ.

20. *"The stars fought from heaven, from their courses they fought against Sisera"* **(Judges 5:20).** Now, begin to declare the following prayers using the name of Jesus Christ after every prayer:

    a. I declare that just as the stars of heaven fought from their courses against Sisera, so shall Jesus Christ manifest as the Star of David to fight all spiritual forces of the heavenlies that are fighting my star;

    b. O Lord, deliver my star from the spirit of *Sisera*;

    c. Every contention over my star is settled today;

    d. The stars of Heaven are overtaking the governments of evil that are against my star.

21. With the Most Precious Blood of Jesus Christ, I cancel every age and timeline set in the satanic clock to cause re-appearance of these problems that are defeated through this prayer, in the name of Jesus Christ, Amen.

22. Thank You, Lord Jesus Christ, for delivering me from the devil and his companions through this prayer.

    a. Sing songs of victory to the Lord;

    b. Offer thanksgiving prayers with **Psalm 96:1-7, Psalm 98:1, Psalm 149.**

23. I cover this prayer with the Most Precious Blood of Jesus Christ (7 times).

Chapter 10

OVERTHROW THE TYRANTS

· · ◆ ◆ ◆ ◆ · · ·

"On the day the Lord gives you relief from your suffering and turmoil and from the harsh labor forced on you, you will take up this taunt against the king of Babylon: How the oppressor has come to an end! How his fury has ended! The Lord has broken the rod of the wicked, the scepter of the rulers, which in anger struck down peoples with unceasing blows, and in fury subdued nations with relentless aggression."
(Isaiah 14:3-6, NKJV)

"How you are fallen from heaven, O Lucifer, son of the morning! How you are cut down to the ground, You who weakened the nations!"
(Isaiah 14:12, NKJV)

(Other suggested Bible passages to read:
2 Kings 13:18-19, 1 Kings 18:41-46, 2 Kings 11:1-4,
Luke 11:21-22, 1 Samuel 30:1-31, 2 Chronicles 20:1-29,
1 Samuel 17:1-58, 1 Kings 18:1-45).

DAY 20

Part 1: Reflection

People say that life is a game. Others, like William Shakespeare, say that the world is a stage and we are all players in the theater of life. However, Job rightly concludes that life is a toil **(Job 7:1)**, a struggle **(Job 14:1)**, and that *"human beings are born to trouble"* **(Job 5:7)**. Job definitely understands that toil is present at every turn of life. This holds true from the smallest scratches we get when we first fall off our bicycle to the profound sorrow we feel when we lose a loved one. Indeed, no one is exempted from the struggles and vicissitudes of life—not even Jesus Christ, who *"Though He was God's Son, He learned through His sufferings to be obedient"* **(Hebrews 5:8, GNT)**.

In His humanity, Jesus suffered the pains of betrayal and of utter rejection by His own people. Jesus, who never rejected anyone **(John 6:37)**, is the most rejected of all people **(Acts 3:14)**. In **John 8:59**, the people *"picked up stones to throw at Him, but Jesus hid Himself and went out of the temple"*—yet, when the hour to face suffering came, Jesus could not escape it. Mary, facing the challenges of an impromptu trip to a strange land with her family, fled to Egypt to escape Herod's brutal plot to kill her son, but when the time of fulfillment of Simeon's prophecy to her came—*"a sword will pierce your own soul too"* **(Luke 2:35)**—she had to face a sword of suffering piercing her heart and her Son's Heart. Neither Mary nor Jesus escaped this moment of suffering.

Before her eyes, she watched cruelty befalling her child! Mary's Son died the most shameful dead—death on the Cross—and she could not help it!—Her wounds were *"as deep as the sea"* **(Lamentations 2:13, NIV)**.

You see, being God's Son did not exempt Jesus from sharing in the suffering of this life. Likewise, being the Mother of Jesus did not exclude Mary from the pains of life! Thus, Jesus prepares our minds about the struggles of life by telling us to *"take up [our] Cross daily and follow"* Him **(Luke 9:23)**. Jesus, by this invitation, is alluding to the fact that a Cross or suffering is part of life. No one, not even the righteous, is exempted from the thorns that life offers—*"you yourselves know that this is what we are destined for"* (**1 Thessalonians 3:3**). Even Prophet Isaiah in his toil and struggle lamented, *"I have labored in vain, I have spent my strength for nothing and vanity"* (**Isaiah 49:4**).

Our tendency is to flee from the wear-and-tear of life— I mean, we desire to avoid the toil at all cost. In today's society, there are medicines to alleviate any pain or suffering we might feel. Yet, pain sprouts again and again because it is interwoven into the very life we live. Job is correct: life is a toil! **(Job 7:1)**.

However, through the struggles we face in this world as Christians, we mature into a deeper knowledge of God, with the conviction that no struggle or toil we go through is bigger than God. The disciples who initially feared the storm later came to trust in Jesus more. As we surrender the troubles we encounter in life to our Lord Jesus Christ, He matures our faith in Him, and even uses the troubles to expose us to our weaknesses whilst developing our godly character.

Jesus came to overthrow the source of our problems, not the problems or their symptoms. The devil or Satan is the source of man's problems. Problems—for instance sickness or poverty— are merely the tool of Satan to afflict God's people. We struggle with these problems. Defeating the problems would have been a great accomplishment, but the enemy would have found another way to wage war against us.

So Jesus went head-to-head against Satan, the cause of man's problems, engaged him in a battle on the old rugged Cross, and after a three-day struggle with death on our behalf, rose victoriously from the grave, having overthrown the devil, to assure the final victory over the enemy. Since Jesus won the battle at Calvary, we are now entitled to share in the spoils of His victory. We appropriate Christ's victory when we anchor on Him, then we see the problems crumbling on their own because Christ has overthrown the master of the problem(s).

The death of Jesus on the old rugged Cross was the ultimate overthrow of the devil and his kingdom. Paradoxically, what looked like defeat—as Jesus hangs on the Cross—brings to us the power, authority, and weapons to overthrow the enemy throughout the ages. The wisdom of the ancient serpent failed him as he watched Jesus use the very weapon of death to bring redemption to the entire mankind! Can you imagine the devil's surprise as he looked at the Cross—that instrument of death and symbol of shame—becoming a symbol of man's redemption?

We are in a warfare against an enemy who seeks to oppress us and keep us from serving the Lord and sharing Him with others. No true believer functions effectively without encountering spiritual battle. Satan and his army of demons will always hurl assaults at the child of God. *"It was allowed to make war on the saints" (Revelation 13:7).* This battle rages on, not only around us, but also within us. There is a fierce conflict over the control of our mind, our heart, and our ultimate destinies. Yet, as **Romans 8:37** tells us, *"In all these things, we are more than conquerors through him who loved us."* In the end, God will surely lift the believer's head over the enemies!

The first conflict in creation started because "Lucifer" sought to overthrow God's very throne in Heaven. Till date, the devil seeks to overthrow the destiny thrones of people's lives as to rule and enslave them. But praise be to God who has given His Son, Jesus Christ, all the power and authority to destroy and overthrow all the power and works of the devil and his kingdom **(John 12:31, 1 John 3:8)**. Jesus brings freedom to all who are troubled and oppressed by the tyrant spirits—provided that they allow Him to be enthroned in their hearts.

The devil is dethroned when we decide to allow Jesus to be enthroned in our hearts. In the military terms, this is somewhat like a spiritual coup d'état in which the headship of your life changes from the devil to Jesus Christ. Again, this spiritual coup could be compared to a medical transplant in which a head is removed (the devil's) but replaced with another Head (Jesus Christ's). I don't need to remind you that this change of headship of your life cannot be done without violence (coup often involves violence). Permit me to softly remind us that *"from the days of John the Baptist until now the kingdom of heaven has suffered violence, and the violent takes it by force"* (Matthew 11:12).

Since we are talking about coup, the need to overthrow the enemy is expedient, I would remind us that coups are best carried out in a midnight, after business hours when most pesky potential obstacles at home are asleep. This translates to the fact that engaging your enemy in a midnight or vigil prayer for a spiritual power-shift and takeover operation is critical for any successful spiritual overthrow.

I hope this midnight prayer-fight clarifies to us why Samson had to wake up in the midnight to attack the Philistines, destroying the gate of their city **(Judges 16:2-3)**. By morning, Samson's voice was thundering in victory in the land of his enemies—much like a successfully executed night coup leads to a morning of new government in which the voice of the leader of the coup plotter charges through the air and being heard as citizens shake the fog of sleep out of their heads.

Likewise, you have to tactfully fight the enemy in a way that you have to be the only voice of victory thundering in the morning. A loosely executed prayer operation meant to overthrow a powerful head is a threat to your whole enterprise. Don't allow them to survive your "coup"! I wish to buttress the dangers of aborted or loosely executed warfare prayer. As I am writing this paragraph, I recall the 1990 execution of 42 coup-plotters (soldiers) who staged an aborted coup in Nigeria in a bid to topple the President. In most cases, aborted coup may result in the Commander-in-Chief arresting the coup plotters together with their family members, and most of their friends in trying to find out what they know about the coup. The consequences of a foiled coup may range from the torturing—in a very chilly and toxic prison—of all the people suspected to be involved in the plot to a brutal execution of everyone. I can't help but think of a surgeon trying to surgically remove a cancer—in this case, the coup plotters—but would have to remove some healthy tissues in order to ensure that all the cancer cells are removed.

The above paragraph simply speaks volumes regarding the spiritual implications of failing to overthrow the enemy sitting on your life and destiny. The bees shall go on a sting spree if you don't destroy them and their beehive (stronghold). The enemy you fought but failed to destroy can come after your family members, your loved ones, or even your business. Do you wonder why your loved ones or those working for you (or your clients) begin to have serious patterned problems after a strong prayer session? Does that sound familiar? My dear, the reason is that either there's an aborted attempt to overthrow the enemies and destroy their stronghold (partial victory) or you were dealing with a case of spiritual reinforcement of the enemies for causing them serious casualties (see Chapter 4 of

Volume 1 of this book on Die-Hard spirits).

In **2 Kings 13:18-19**, Elisha *"said to the king of Israel, 'Strike the ground'; so he struck three times, and stopped. And the man of God was angry with him, and said, 'You should have struck five or six times; then you would have struck Syria till you had destroyed it! But now you will strike Syria only three times'"* (NKJV) .Why was Elisha angry with the King? He was angry because the King had the opportunity to strike the ground *"five or six times"* for a complete victory to overthrow the powerful Syria, but he struck the ground *"only three times"* and had loosely executed prayer operation. Many of us pray but we don't strike enough to have breakthroughs. Elijah prayed seven times before the heavy rainfall that broke the three-and-half years of drought poured down **(1 Kings 18:41-46)**. Elijah had fully executed prayer operation that changed the economic climate of his nation. Pray very hard enough to see the results of your victory. You can change the spiritual and economic climates around you on your knees!

It was *"when Athaliah, Ahaziah's mother, saw that her son was dead, [that] she set about to destroy all the royal family"* (2 Kings 11:1). However, it was when Jehoiada led a coup d'état against Athaliah, supported by the captains of the temple, that Athaliah was dethroned and executed (2 Kings11:4)— and then peace reigned in the land. This is the beauty of a successful spiritual coup plot—Peace! Again, I emphasize that you should not allow the enemy to survive your coup operation as you pray! Loosely executed prayer operations are dangerous!

Brethren, if the devil does not know you as a fighter or a tactical coup plotter, he will treat you as a civilian— ordinary, powerless, and inexperienced folks! To tell you the truth: the devil doesn't fear Boy Scouts or Girl Guides, but dread real soldiers of Christ. My dear, Satan doesn't care so much if you're a Christian as long as you don't act like a soldier of Christ! The devil fears fire-brand Christians because he knows that they have the backup of Heaven—and that Jesus Christ, the Commander of the Supreme Headquarters of Heavenly Council, and the General of the Heavenly Armies **(Revelation 19:14)** will deploy His armies to fight for His people. The kingdom of darkness knows that very well.

The tyrant spirits are not concerned about your freedom. It is Jesus Christ who wants you free. Although true freedom is free, but it will not come cheaply—this is why you must fight for it! True freedom from the tyrants cannot be appropriated without a spiritual battle. In order to be free, the tyrant's regime in our life must be overthrown, and this requires a massive warfare. We must understand that freedom is not an inherent natural birthright; for, it comes with a cost: It cost Jesus His life to give us freedom; it will cost us carrying the cross.

Our spiritual enemies have power, and will not stop fighting with the power in their possession. They are determined to disarm you or, at the worst, kill your destiny. You may need to be reminded that the devil doesn't depart from people on his own accord nor retire willingly, unless they are disarmed, dethroned and forced out by prayers. Jesus Himself encountered personal oppositions; He battled with Satan and defeated him.

Intense bombardment of prayers breaks and overthrows the power of the tyrants, disabling their tentacles that hold people in spiritual oppression. Once the power of the spiritual tyrants is broken off from your life, it clears the atmosphere for the power of God to be felt freely and powerfully. How can we overthrow and overturn the structures that are holding many captive if not by way of prayer? How can you overpower the strongman and recover your blessings if not by the power of prevailing prayer? When you overpower the strongman with your prayers, then you plunder his spoils having overthrown him **(Luke 11:21-22)**. Prayer is the key to overthrow the forces of darkness.

Therefore, we must, by our prayers, overthrow the thrones of iniquity that are ruling the earth and influencing the Church. When our prayer rises, powers of darkness and all satanic structures begin to break, and every pattern of generational bondage that has stopped families from experiencing the blessings of God will begin to collapse. We ought to use the art of prayer to recover the spoils the enemy has taken from us. There would be no restoration without fervent prayer!

The only institution on earth that has the power to break the enemy's strongholds is the Church. A praying Church has the authority to overthrow the kingdom of darkness, and transfer the inheritance of nations into the storehouse of the Lord—after all *"the sinner's wealth is laid up for the righteous"* **(Proverbs 13:22b)**. The importance of a praying Church cannot be overstressed! The Church must change into a vibrant, fire-filled army that marches forward with a determined mission to overthrow the systems of the devil. I hope you are determined to overthrow the invisible forces sitting on your throne.

LET US PRAY!

1. Reflect on how this reflection on "Overthrow the Tyrants" ministers to you.

2. Pray the Saint Michael the Archangel prayer (see page 17).

3. Pray the Anima Christi prayer (see page 18).

4. Pray Psalm 10 (a prayer for the overthrow of the wicked).

5. Lord God, Your Word promises in Jeremiah 1:10— *"See, to-day I appoint you over nations and over kingdoms, to pluck up*

and to pull down, to destroy and to overthrow, to build and to plant."

a. I ..... *(pick from the following list)* the spiritual tyrants attacking my life, in the name of Jesus Christ.

- Overthrow
- Overcome
- Overpower
- Overturn
- Disable
- Roast

- Pull down
- Destroy
- Break
- Smite
- Dismantle
- Paralyze

- Pluck up
- Set on fire
- Render impotent
- Crush
- Disorganize
- Suffocate

b. I scatter the spiritual forces that are joined together against me and my family, in the name of Jesus Christ.

c. I bind and rebuke all demonic reinforcements sent by the kingdom of darkness to attack my life, in the name of Jesus Christ;

d. *"Let them be put to shame and dismayed forever; let them perish in disgrace"* **(Psalm 83:17)**—in the name of Jesus Christ;

e. I release confusion in their camp. I command them to begin to attack each other according to the order of **(2 Chronicles 20:23)** —in the name of Jesus Christ;

f. I command every wall erected by the enemy against me and my family to be destroyed now **(Ezekiel 13:14)**— in the name of Jesus Christ;

g. I command every altar erected by the enemy against me and my family to be destroyed now **(Hosea10:2)**—in the name of Jesus Christ;

h. I break and destroy every demonic blockage and barrier of the enemy to hinder the will and plans of God for me and my family—in the name of Jesus Christ.

6. I command evil thrones of iniquity to collapse now, in the name of Jesus Christ. Make the following intercessory prayers (in the name of Jesus Christ):

a. Pray to overthrow thrones of iniquity in the Church:
    i. Pray for the priests, pastors and the religious;
    ii. Pray for the seminarians and over the seminaries (and your parish);
    iii. Pray that God's Throne be established in the hearts of people;
    iv. Pray that the Church rises into a new glory.
b. Pray to overthrow thrones of iniquity in the Government, School system, hospital and health systems, media, and the society at large;
c. Pray for a tremendous shift in the spirit that brings about global repentance and revival;
d. Pray against every form of worship that exalts Satan.

7. *"Then he said, 'Take the arrows'; so he took them. And he said to the king of Israel, 'Strike the ground'; so he struck three times, and stopped. And the man of God was angry with him, and said, 'You should have struck five or six times; then you would have struck Syria till you had destroyed it! But now you will strike Syria only three times'"* (2 Kings 13:19, NKJV). Be very aggressive now since you want to overthrow your enemy. Strike the ground many times (note that each strike on the ground weakens your enemy. Strike many times for complete victory!) Make the following prayers in the name of Jesus christ:
    a. According to the mystery of Elisha, I strike the ground (*keep striking the ground with every seriousness in you*) till the enemy is completely destroyed;
    b. O Lord Jesus, let every strike on the ground cause terrible earthquake and shattering thunder in the kingdom of darkness.

8. Thank the Lord and cover this prayer with the Most Precious Blood of Jesus Christ (7 times).

DAY 21

Part 2: Warfare Prayers

Note:
- You are about to execute a spiritual coup (coup d'état) operation to overthrow your enemy and take over his estate.

1. Offer songs to the Lord as the Holy Spirit directs you.

2. Blood of Jesus Christ cleanse me from my sins (confess them).
   a. Use **Psalm 51** to ask God for the forgiveness of your sins;
   b. I am sorry for the ways I have cooperated with the spiritual tyrants knowingly or unknowingly to achieve their missions in my life and family;
   c. As a society, we are sorry for the ways we have cooperated with the tyrants to achieve their missions in the society.

3. Pray the prayer of Saint Michael the Archangel (see page 17).

4. Pray the Anima Christi prayer (see page 18).

5. I cover myself and my household, and the environment of this prayer with the Most Precious Blood of Jesus Christ (7 times).

6. I confess with my mouth that:
   a. There is no condition too difficult for my God to change;
   b. There is no environment too difficult for my God to operate;
   c. There is no enemy too strong for my God to overthrow.

7. O Lord Jesus, spoil the tyrants agenda, program and mission in my life and family, in the Church, marriages and the entire society, in the name of Jesus Christ I pray.

8. Lord Jesus, I trust in You to give me victory over the tyrants that hinder my relationship with You and my witness for You.

9. Lord Jesus, make me indomitable so that no earthly trial can subdue me, in the name of Jesus Christ.

10. Lord Jesus, You promised in **Psalm 119:50** to bring me life and peace in the midst of life's storms. Therefore, Lord Jesus, give me comfort in my times of distress, in the name of Jesus Christ.

11. At the command of Joshua, the sun and the moon stood still **(Joshua 10:12-13)**. So at my command, let every evil storm stand still in the name of Jesus Christ.

12. In the name of Jesus Christ, I lead spiritual tyrants *"away stripped and overthrow [their] officials long established"* **(Job 12:19)**.

13. I command every evil power sitting on my blessings to catch fire, in the name of Jesus Christ.

14. I can never labor in vain, in the name of Jesus Christ.

15. I shall walk this year in victory and liberty of the spirit, in the name of Jesus Christ.

16. I cancel all appointments with sorrow, tragedy and evil cry this year, in the name of Jesus Christ.

17. Anything I have waited for a long time up till now, shall be miraculously delivered to me this year, in the name of Jesus Christ.

18. This year, I enter into covenant with ----- *(pick from the following),* in the name of Jesus Christ.

    - Fruitfulness
    - Kairos moment
    - Good harvest
    - Success
    - Favor
    - Grace
    - Promotion
    - Blessings
    - Victory

19. This year, all obstacles on my way of progress shall be dismantled, and I shall not give in to despair, in the name of Jesus Christ.

20. I recover all my confiscated and stolen goods, in the name of Jesus Christ.

21. Holy Spirit, shake down and break into pieces every weight of foundational stronghold, padlock, and chain limiting my progress in life, in the name of Jesus Christ.

22. I reclaim all my trapped blessings, in the name of Jesus Christ.

23. O Lord Jesus, send Your Angels to roll away every stone placed upon my progress, in the name of Jesus Christ.

24. I command every doorway and ladder of satanic invasion into my life to be closed, in the name of Jesus Christ.

25. Thank You, Lord Jesus Christ, for giving me the grace to overtake all the invisible enemies that are fighting me.
    a. Sing songs of victory to the Lord;
    b. Offer thanksgiving prayers with **Psalms 34:1-3,** and **Psalms 67:3-7.**

26. I cover this prayer with the Most Precious Blood of Jesus Christ (7 times).

EPILOGUE

···◆ ◆ ◆ ◆···

Here comes the end. I am glad that you made it to the end of this book. You have just concluded a spiritual warfare operation. The fact that you've made it this far is a good indication that you are a sure winner in your spiritual battle. So, congratulations! As I look back and reflect on all the obstacles that rose up to stop this book from being written, I can't help but say, "God, You have fought the battle and given your servant victory." I'd like to use this epilogue to make some final remarks on this book, *"The Invisible War"*.

I woke up this morning with a beautiful and peaceful weather greeting me—a peace that accompanies me as I pen down this epilogue: A peace I believe you are already experiencing in your spirit having been delivered from the power of darkness—or having defeated the invisible forces that are fighting your Christian journey. Having gone through this book, I believe that you are this book's defense attorney: A testament that this book is fully loaded with information and prayers that everyone needs in order to stay ahead of the enemy.

After publishing my first book, *"War against Python and Snake Spirits"*, people who prayed with the book felt blessed from the many miracles and diverse testimonies that resulted from their prayer warfare. With this motivation, I began a second edition of the book. But not long after I started writing it, I heard the Lord's voice saying, "Tyrant". This word resonated in my spirit for a couple of weeks. It didn't take long for me to discern what Heaven wanted me to do: The Lord wanted me to write a book that deals with spiritual tyrants. My head appeared bland on this subject, but with prayer and God's grace, the Holy Spirit guided me into writing what you have in your hands now. When I was writing the chapter on "Weapons against the Spiritual Tyrants" (Chapter 2 of this book), the Lord asked me to develop it into another book. As a result, I started writing the two books concurrently. The second book is titled, *"The Warrior's Weapons."* Reading and praying fervently with these companion books and with *"War against Python and Snake Spirits"* would make you a warrior in spiritual battles!

Never in any human history has there been an outbreak of demonic hostilities like ours. The horror we see in our time confirms the preaching that the devil is indeed all out to fight the people of God. It's time to put the spiritual enemies on notice! This book is a weapon to keep them on notice. Keep using this book to push back the invisible enemies rising against you. I encourage you to get copies of this book for your friends. Use it in the Churches, prayer groups, Bible study groups, or for family prayers. Together, as we pray, we shall cause serious casualties to the kingdom of darkness. Keep your armor on, and rejoice that someday soon our struggle will be over forever!

Due to the overflow of inspirational graces granted while writing this book, I am articulating this work as a series. While the Volume 2 you are holding in your hands focused on confronting the spiritual tyrants, the Volume 1 deals with the nature and the characteristics of the spiritual tyrants. I encourage you to get the Volume 1 of this book (and check out for other volumes in the series). Stay tuned!

God bless you!

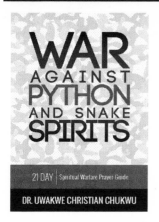

War Against Python and Snake Spirits

The first Biblical prophecy in Genesis 3:15 simply reveals a salient truth: There is a spiritual hostility and conflict between the righteous and the devil, the ancient serpent. God wants us to engage the ancient serpent in a battle. He wants us to use the authority He has given to us to smash the serpent's head! Unfortunately, so many people of God are bound by demonic forces but do not know how to be free. The proliferation of python and snake spirits in this end time has resulted in an epidemic of people living in spiritual bondage. These python and snake spirits have aggressive appetite for destinies to swallow! War Against Python And Snake Spirits is an attempt to address this problem.

The Warrior's Weapons (Volume 1 & 2)

Never in the history of mankind has there been an era of war like ours. We could smell war in the air. While the media reminds us of physical wars, the struggles we go through everyday remind us of spiritual wars. In a sense, it seems that there is an outbreak of demonic hostilities. Now that we know that we are at war, so what? What are we going to do about it? If we are to survive these trying times in which we live, it is imperative that we learn how to effectively use the weapons of warfare against the devil and his companions.

In this book, you have everything you need to become armed and dangerous against every adversary that threatens you and your destiny. The book presents strategic weapons in our spiritual arsenal and how they are to be used against the kingdom of darkness.

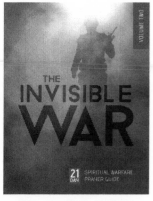

The Invisible War (Volume 1 & 2)

Spiritual war is a fierce battle that is not visible to the ordinary eyes. The war is invisible, but the impact is real. All of us are in the midst of this war which rages underneath the earth, inside the waters, in the air, and in the heavenlies. The battle goes on irrespective of whether we know it or not, or whether we believe it or not. There is no break in the war, no causal leave, and no cease-fire! This occurs every single day both during the day and night. The Invisible War is a fire-loaded warfare book prayerfully packaged to make you dangerous against every spiritual adversary that threatens your destiny. It is written to be engaging as you find in it a blend of real-life experiences, history, Scriptures, storytelling, and prayers.